I Hid It under the Sheets

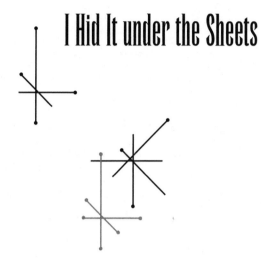

Sports and American Culture Series

Bruce Clayton, Editor

I Hid It under the Sheets

Growing Up with Radio

Gerald Eskenazi

University of Missouri Press

Columbia and London

Library of Congress Cataloging-in-Publication Data

Eskenazi, Gerald.
    I hid it under the sheets : growing up with radio / Gerald Eskenazi.
        p. cm. — (Sports and American culture series)
    Summary: "Personal narrative that documents radio's impact on American
culture and values in the late 1930s, 1940s, and the early 1950s. Mentions the
Lone Ranger, The Fat Man, and The Answer Man, and shows how important
radio was to immigrants seeking to become a part of the American experience"—Provided by publisher.
    Includes index.
    ISBN-13: 978-0-8262-1620-5 (alk. paper)
    ISBN-10: 0-8262-1620-X (alk. paper)
    1. Radio broadcasting—United States—History. 2. Radio broadcasting—
Social aspects—United States. I. Title. II. Series.
    PN1991.3.U6E85 2005
    302.23'44'0973—dc22
                                                2005018184

∞™ This paper meets the requirements of the
American National Standard for Permanence of Paper
for Printed Library Materials, Z39.48, 1984.

Designer: Jennifer Cropp
Typesetter: foleydesign.net
Printer and binder: The Maple-Vail Book Manufacturing Group
Typefaces: Minion and Runic

To my wife, Roz, who listened when I did—
and was part of my life even before we met.

Contents

Acknowledgments

I suppose this book is a paean to my childhood, and to my mother. For radio was my constant companion along with her.

Proust longed for his madeleines, and Citizen Kane for his Rosebud. What triggers these remembrances of radio—even more intriguing, why do they seem so fabulous the farther away we get?

I did not try to get a big picture of childhood, but a snapshot of one aspect of it, an aspect that after all these years still evokes a smile and a stream of consciousness that could take up most of my mornings.

The funny thing is—it happens to everyone I know when I talk to them about the once-upon-a-time of radio. It doesn't matter who they are, or what they're doing now.

Anyone who ever listened to a radio in my era of growing up—the 1940s and 1950s—has exactly the same smile, the same remembrances. We can recite the same commercials, the same signature narratives: "Who knows what evil lurks in the hearts of men? The Shadow knows."

I asked Colin Powell about it just days after he announced his intention to resign as secretary of state in the George W. Bush administration. No problem. Powell started to talk about how important radio had been to him as a boy in the Bronx.

Just about that same time right after World War II, Tom Brokaw was listening to radio in the open Plains, imagining a world out there beyond Sioux City, Iowa. "This is great stuff," Brokaw told me as he contemplated those days he turned the dial. Somewhere east of Brokaw's prairie existence, Bill Parcells was fascinated by the incredible world of make-believe heroes. A prelude, perhaps, to his remarkable ability to coax football players?

They happened to have been three of the most prominent of my contemporaries who shared their radio thoughts with me. All of us also listened to that ubiquitous actor, Mason Adams, who invited me up for coffee one morning to talk about what it was like being the voice of so many of the characters we heard on the radio.

I had started to look back at the significance of what is now called old-time radio in shared moments with my wife, Rosalind. Among her many theories is that while radio affected everyone who listened, it had a truly magical impact on people like her and me—each an only child. Since she is always right, I must agree.

But all of my friends and family know what I'm talking about, too, in mentioning *The Green Hornet,* or *Superman,* or the cigarette commercials. Everyone I spoke to had a memory that wasn't just a random thread, but that was significant in their lives. For radio was a part of our acculturation—giving us values, a hint of literature, a window to culture. It also enveloped us in fantasy, and took us away from the moment when we might be doing something so mundane as homework. Of course, it helps when an editor-in-chief knows exactly what you're talking about. Thus, I got lucky that Beverly Jarrett not only was listening when I was, but encouraged me to go ahead and write about those times.

So to everyone who ever looked up in the sky for Superman, or worried about B.O., or hid under the sheets when *Inner Sanctum* came on the air—thanks for tuning in.

I Hid It under the Sheets

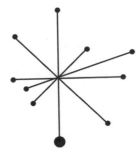

Chapter 1

The Box

Back in the 1940s in Brooklyn, where I lived with my mother, grand-parents, and uncle, we had a Freed-Eisemann radio. It was a piece of furniture on four legs, and higher than a twenty-seven-inch television set is today. And when I was a bad boy, my grandfather would remove one of the radio tubes, which was four inches high and as wide as a lightbulb, from the back of the set, and I could not listen to my shows. That was my punishment.

But when I listened, the box itself had a mystical aura, as if there were tiny worlds back there among the huge tubes.

Indeed, the radio itself was an object of wonder, not merely for the sounds it produced and the transportation it provided. It had a massive knob in the middle, with a pointer. The pointer was flush against the dial itself, its numbers (AM only) running from 540 to a stratospheric 1700. There was a lightbulb in there somewhere illuminating the dial.

The dials' lower reaches and upper reaches were for barely audible exotica—stations broadcasting in Italian, or emanating from Canada! Or maybe even exotic Cleveland. Late at night, if you listened very closely and turned the knob very, very slowly, you might be able to pick up something foreign-sounding between 710 (WOR, Mutual) and 770 (WJZ, ABC). This space between the big local stations was a no-man's land. But at about 730 on the dial, I could discern French spoken, probably from Quebec.

And on Sunday mornings, somewhere high on the dial above 1050 (WHN), I could hear the joyous shouts of Gospel music and screaming preachers and rhythmic organ playing. On some of these high-numbered stations I could pick up an announcer speaking Yiddish, or a Slavic language I imagined somehow had been transported from overseas instead of from a neighborhood studio in Brooklyn. Maybe even somebody's basement, for all I knew.

I never saw a punch thrown, or a glass shatter, or a blood-smeared shirt as I listened on the radio. Nor did I know Barbara Stanwyck's hairstyle as she overacted in *Sorry, Wrong Number* on Lux Radio Theatre. And I had no idea how corpulent Happy Felton was as he dropped ten silver dollars that jangled into a Sheffield's Milk bottle on *Guess Who.* (Yes, ten bucks was what you won on that show.)

Instead, I imagined it all—from Sky King's plane that swooped low over the outlaws' lairs, to the galloping white horse that transported the Lone Ranger, to Clark Kent in the ubiquitous phone booth changing into Superman, to the Black Beauty, the souped-up car that carried the Green Hornet and his faithful Filipino servant, Kato—who, according to a wide-ranging legend, was Japanese before Dec. 7, 1941. After that date, it was said, he morphed into a Filipino. Actually, that never happened, but people today swear they heard him described as a Japanese—just as so many claim they were listening to a football game in the Polo Grounds between the Giants and the Brooklyn Dodgers that fateful day and heard the announcement summoning a Colonel Donovan to the box office to pick up an important message. "Wild Bill" Donovan, an aide to President Franklin Roosevelt, and who soon was to head the Office of Strategic Services—the forerunner of the CIA—then heard the news of the Japanese attack.

Oh, I didn't need a moving image to know what Ivan Shark's malevolent daughter, Fury, looked like as she conspired against Captain Midnight, and I could taste the Wheaties, the Breakfast of Champions, and its healthful vitamins which gave Jack Armstrong the strength to save himself from the fast-approaching treacherous rapids.

When the shows ended their fifteen-minute stint with a cliff-hanger, I had my secret decoder badge ready to get the word on tomorrow's renewal: it would be something tantalizing, such as "Danger in Cave."

I see now that these characters actually were part of an extended family—mine. They filled in the empty spaces in my life: the father (or fatherly types), a sister, a brother. With them, all things were possible. They treated one another—the good guys, that is—with compassion, good humor, and manners. They did things together, and they did them well.

They were virtually all twentieth-century heroic figures, created at the time of the sixty-mile-an-hour locomotive, airplanes that could whisk you coast-to-coast in sixteen hours, inventions such as the X-ray (not to mention the two-way wrist radio). Like America, like the skyward rise of the big cities' tall buildings, the uses and possibilities of technology, electricity, the combustion engine—all were limitless.

In real life, in the postwar (the Second World War, of course) years, it seemed that every week a new speed record was set—either in an airplane, a train, or a car. These record-setters were famous, from Jacqueline Cochrane, always described as "the blonde aviatrix," who became the first woman to set this record or that record, to flight crews from the military, who went from London to New York, say, in record time.

I remember a front-page story in the *Daily News* describing how we actually made contact with the moon for the first time—via a radar beam bounced off that big rock and whose images reverberated back to earth. That was news.

How impressed I was with the daily breakthroughs in technology that emerged at the end of World War II—among them, the ballpoint pen! An early ad, I recall, said that one pen would write for two years. Indeed, when Gimbels department store in New York put them on sale, barely two months after the Japanese surrendered, ten thousand ballpoints were sold that day—at $12.50 apiece. Our fantasies were coming true.

If a pen could write forever, if man could touch the moon—even electronically—if you could have dinner in New York and breakfast in Paris, then why not have a radio hero whose secret handshakes told the good guys from the bad, or who could drive a car at breakneck speed after thugs through darkened streets, or who could even—even—take off his glasses and be able to see through brick walls (not to mention, be able to blow them down)?

Why, indeed? Remember, I had a coal cellar in our house, which was built before the war—World War I that is. Thinking about coal as a fuel today—why, it's almost as if you're contemplating a prehistoric dragonfly caught in a piece of amber. Yet, that wasn't the only old-fashioned thing about my house in the 1940s. In many ways, it resembled the interior of a house of the 1920s, with all its trappings, before the surge of consumerism and the avalanche of modernity overtook America.

There was our kitchen, for example. It had an icebox. That's right—a block of ice sat in its container atop a wooden box, connected to a series of coils that cooled the food. It was, I believe, a six-cubic-foot box.

Once a week, maybe more often, some guy named Tony or Sal would pull up in a truck in front of the house, take out a small pick axe, and chip out a fifty-pound block of ice from the huge slabs on the back of the truck, which were covered with a burlap tarpaulin. Then he'd put a smaller piece of burlap over his left shoulder, and hoist a block of ice onto it. Only slightly stooped, he'd walk up the flight of stairs to our apartment and place the ice onto the box.

The icebox had a drain for the melted water, which had to be emptied by hand into the sink. I don't think we had ice cubes—at least, not until we eventually got a real electric refrigerator with room for a couple of trays and not much else in its so-called freezer compartment.

Except for the overhead light, we had nothing electric in the kitchen—not even a toaster. In the morning, we made toast on a contraption that had been bought for ten cents years earlier in a Woolworth's 5-and-10. It was a trapezoidal metal toaster that was placed directly on top of an open flame on the gas stove. My grandmother didn't believe in an electric range. What if there were a blackout? she reasoned. Similarly, our first refrigerator also was powered by gas, not electricity. The toaster on top of the range was enclosed, but had a thin railing on the bottom of each of the four sides on which you put a slice of bread. Then you turned on a low flame on a top burner and waited for the side of the bread closest to the toaster to turn brown. When it did, you turned the bread over. It was perfect toast—when it didn't burn.

For most of the Second World War, we did not have a telephone, either. On those rare occasions when we actually received a phone call, it came to the candy store across the street. There always were kids hanging out at the store, and if someone called us—by dialing the pay phone in the store—one of the youngsters was dispatched to ring our bell and get my mother or grandparents.

Toward the end of the war, we finally got a phone. The number was Applegate 7-3605. The first two letters—AP—were part of the prefix. Every telephone prefix had a name—the most famous, of course, was Pennsylvania, as in the Glenn Miller hit, "Pennsylvania 6-5000," which was the phone number of the Hotel Pennsylvania, across the street from Penn Station. John O'Hara's novel *Butterfield 8* also had an evocative ring to it, so to speak. There were no area codes, and if we wanted to dial outside of the five boroughs—an event that would be cause for an extended discussion within the family, something alien and creating as much excitement as taking an airplane ride—we telephoned the operator. A car? A ridiculous notion. Not one of my friends had one, either. Everyone took the subway to work, and rode the bus or train to visit family on weekends.

In the midst of this old—and, let me admit, somewhat low-income— milieu stood our radio. This was my one true electronic connection to midcentury America. Well, in the summer, there was one electric fan for the family. And as the gift-giving season approached—Chanukah wasn't that far from Christmas—I would wish each year for a set of electric trains. I never got one. My mother did own a box camera, a Kodak you held against your chest for stability, and sighted by looking down at the viewfinder, on top of the camera. The grocer's landlord, an ancient, bearded man who lived over the store, actually had a television set. He invited me over one night to watch this wonder. The screen was a little bigger than a pack of cigarettes, and had a magnifying glass over it. No matter. What was behind the curved, distorted image was fascinating in black and white. My first glimpse of television. I was eleven years old, I was sitting on a couch, and I was watching someone dancing. Soon, I saw another television set.

My father occasionally took me to places where his friends hung out on the Lower East Side of Manhattan, an area hardly changed in the fifty years since the turn of the century, when immigrants brought their huge families to live in two-bedroom apartments, slept outside on the fire escape in the summer heat, and did their shopping from the pushcarts on the streets below. My father was born in Istanbul. His mother was from Marseilles. Perhaps that's why his friends called him "Frenchie." Or maybe it was his good looks. With his mustache, he had an uncanny resemblance to Clark Gable. There was a rakishness about him, but also a terrible temper. In any social situation, I wondered how long it would be before he got in a quarrel with someone. But he and his friends enjoyed a good laugh in a smoke-filled bar, filled with old men from the old country. They often sat opposite each other playing backgammon. They smoked tobacco from a water pipe known as a hookah. Some even wore a tasseled fez, which by then had been outlawed in Turkey, but which for traditionalists was still a symbol of their manhood. In these dim, post–World War II enclaves, I used to watch wrestling on television with my father. Every table had a bowl of pine nuts in the center, and the men drank a traditional milky liquor called *raki*. "Lion's milk," they joked. But they were serious about their wrestling, which was on four nights a week. The Turks, after all, loved wrestling. Their national sport remains wrestling even today. So what if the wrestling they were watching on those ten-inch screens was a fraud? The place was noisy, there was smoke, there was *raki* and laughter. Just like the old country.

But I was part of another network of kids, rich and poor. The radio kids. Thus, like school kids all over America, we all went inside our houses at a quarter to 5 in the early evening to listen to the kids' shows. For in fifteen minutes, the first of the night's adventures would begin.

Radio.

Around the country, millions of children like me, like my friends, would spend the next hours listening to an imagination-expanding series of broadcasts over the radio that would transport us to other places: the frontier towns of the Lone Ranger; Captain Midnight, Jack Armstrong (the All-American Boy), Superman, Little Orphan Annie, Don Winslow of the Navy, Tom Mix.

When you consider that a kid my age, say nine or ten or eleven, woke up at 7:30 in the morning and went to bed at 9 p.m., then fully one-sixth of my day was spent listening to these adventure serials. And that doesn't include the snippets of late-night radio I sneaked under the blanket after they were over, or the morning shows such as Arthur Godfrey and His Friends, or Don McNeill's Breakfast Club, or Dorothy and Dick, before going to school (or, staying home from school just to listen to the soap operas).

My late-night adventures began when my mother brought home a contraption the size of a two-slice toaster—a Motorola radio that was AC-DC and portable. Even as the 1950s dawned, there were places in America that did not have alternating-current electricity. Instead, they used direct current—hence, radios that were compatible with both. And "portable"? The battery was the size and thickness of a pack of cigarettes, and quite dense. She placed the radio on top of a night table. It was not radio as I knew it. This was not a handsome piece of furniture. It hardly had any tubes. Why, you could actually pick it up. And then she turned it on. My disappointment was immense. For this was not theater. Sitting in my living room, looking at and listening to the four-legged behemoth that was so prominent, with bass so deep you could feel the machine vibrate—why, that was a radio. When I sat down to listen to the Freed-Eisemann, I was in the same state of anticipation as going to a movie theater. Adventure awaited.

Still, there was no way that four-foot-high radio was going to make it under my sheets. Thus, the Motorola found a place in my heart, and my bed, as I listened past the squawking static to pick up further adventures.

The serials all died similar deaths—zapped by the glare of the television tubes that obliterated them fifty years ago. But their run, from the mid 1930s until the early 1950s, captivated a generation and still holds me.

One-sixth of an impressionable child's life—how could it not affect you in later years? How it affected me. These impressions are what I remember and what impacted me. It is not an attempt to be encyclopedic. It is an attempt to discover how that box shaped me, and the effect it had on the world around me—indeed, the world around all of us.

Chapter 2

Home

Imagine that there was a time in America when a child sat next to a radio and simply listened. But not just listen, be enthralled and know that this time was his alone, that he was part of the vortex of drama unfolding inside the radio's innards.

In my pre-teen years, the only radio in the house was in the living room, so I would sit on the floor, my head next to the big box, and listen. All by myself. By then, around 5 p.m., my grandmother already was preparing dinner. My grandfather was virtually deaf, and he would make the effort to listen to radio only for special occasions—Sunday night, when Walter Winchell was on, or after supper at night during the week, when the news was presented by Gabriel Heatter, who began every program with, "Ah, there's good news tonight!" (And whose daughter, Maida Heatter, is the noted cookbook author.)

My mother, meanwhile, was on her way home from work, riding the subway, and my Uncle Arthur was in England during the war, and then in school when he returned from overseas.

My mother worked sewing women's hats, an industry that once upon a time was quite important in New York. She got paid by the hat—piece work, it was called—and the more she worked, the more she earned. So she often worked until 6 o'clock at night, as well as on Saturdays when the busy season was under way. It meant that she was never there to see me in a school play, or when I captured my public school spelling championship and came close to being a finalist for the National Spelling Bee. Nor did she ever meet any of my teachers, or know my friends' mothers.

In fact, there was an air of mystery about her—not to me, but to other women, the teachers I had, the mothers of my friends, the owners of the local stores. They would ask me questions about the type of job she had—imagine, she took the subway to work!—and how old she was, and did she see her former husband. I know this is just my take on it, trying to remember things all these years later, but I had the sense that there was also an admiration, a sense of . . . what, wonderment? . . . that a woman could be on her own, not be enveloped by events, make a life on her own, for her child. There were moments, in fact, when I detected jealousy in the questions about her. That was at once curious and uplifting to me. For while I had always longed for what I had considered the ideal mom-and-pop family—the kind, you know, that radio offered—I also understood that I had something special going on. Indeed, when a new friend's mother invariably would ask about my mother, it was followed by implied pity for me, and yet with strong curiosity about my mother. What no one understood, however, was the loneliness. My loneliness.

So during those golden early evening hours, it was just me and the radio.

Little did I know that in far-off Queens, a blonde girl with curly hair was also listening by herself. Her name was Rosalind. Like me, my wife-to-be was an only child. Her mother also worked. Her father did too. My wife-to-be was alone in her house from the time she came home from school at 3 o'clock until 6 p.m. She was eight years old. So when it was time to go into the early evening fantasy-land of the radio serial, both of us were alone by our radios.

I think, now, that we were simply looking for friends.

"Only children," she says now, "probably listened to radio more than those who had brothers or sisters."

Those of us who are only children don't have anyone to bounce fears and dreams off of—or fantasies. I could tell my friends the next day about what I had heard, but I didn't share the live moment of the serials with them. This I did alone, as did my wife. Only later, many years later, did we share this with each other.

But I'll say this about being home alone. While there may have been a longing for that elusive family structure, at the same time I was imbued with an ability to act independently. I walked to school by myself in the second and third grades. I took the bus (a nickel) all over Brooklyn, and by the time I was ten years old, I often would ride the subway with just friends. After all, what could happen to a youngster on a New York City subway?

Today, of course, when I pass a cute child being wheeled by his mother (or, increasingly in Manhattan, by a nanny), I resist the urge to pat his head. Who knows what crime I could be accused of?

The radio itself was a cocoon, with its fabric covering the speaker—a sort of curtain separating me from the world inside. Oz-like, you might say. I would touch the wood of the radio and feel a slight vibration as someone spoke, and I put my ear next to the hidden speaker to see if I could detect someone whispering in the background. After all, there was this hidden world back there, and there had to be more than one voice at a time. Of course, I heard these other voices, didn't I? I'm sure I did.

I was completely enveloped in my radio universe. Take the world of *Captain Midnight.* It began with a sonorous-voiced announcer intoning "Cap-tain Mid-niiiight," and the portentous peals of a clock that sounded like Big Ben, and then the drone of a low-flying airplane. Clearly, the airplane was part of the mystique of this show, if not the entire era: a plane connoted mystery, adventure, possibility, as if just being transported someplace else by flying somehow changed the dynamics of human life. An airplane ride has no such meaning today. It is another means of transportation. There are no myths attached to it. But you have to understand that, for me, everything on radio was almost-mythic—we didn't even have a car, or a telephone. Nor did I have a father, at least not in the house.

Because *Captain Midnight* conjured up night and fog and who knows what other fairy tales, the opening segment scared me. But then suddenly there'd be light organ strains, and one of Captain Midnight's bevy of young assistants—super-heroes in training?—would say something brightly, and the show would begin.

When my children were of an age when they listened intently to my bedtime stories, I told them about old radio programs. One of those was *Captain Midnight,* and its somber beginning.

As time went by—that is, as they got older—I had the suspicion they didn't always believe my stories of childhood, in which I invariably got in trouble by being bad, and somehow extricated myself.

As I write this, it suddenly occurs to me, for the first time, what I had been doing—I had been reciting my own radio show! My life as a serial.

The stories would open with some enjoyable moment—I'm standing in the kitchen of my grandmother's farm, looking out the window at a deer coming out of the woods—and suddenly I hear her scream.

Or, I was playing punchball—a street game—and I whacked the soft rubber ball harder than I ever had in my life. But then there was the over-head power line in the way of the trajectory.

I even had a story about the spelling competition when I was in the sixth grade. And how I was sailing along, spelling words like "Repub-licanism," when suddenly they asked me to spell "television."

I failed. I explained to my saddened children that the reason I couldn't spell it was because we were too poor to have a television set at home. Thus, never having watched television, how was I to spell it? They loved that story. And they learned, at an early age, how to spell "television." No "i" after "l."

All the stories I told, however, were true. And those that weren't—well, they should have been. These were all stories with a moral of some kind, something instructive that made Ellen, Mark, or Mike think. Sometimes, however, the stories did not have happy endings, unlike my radio days.

Yet, I think that having listened to radio, I was able to construct these playlets at night: knowing when to pause for effect, understanding how to introduce characters, and then coming to a dramatic ending. In the rare moments when the ending escaped me, why, I'd simply make it a cliff-hanger—I'd serialize it, and promise to tell them the ending the next night.

Because they couldn't envision the fact that I had once run away from home, or that I had been sent to the principal's office—or even that I had grown up without a television set—I think they were also skeptical of the radio shows I told them about. It was, finally, inconceivable that I grew up without television, but instead planted myself in front of a box and simply sat and listened. My children's radio experience was altogether different: they listened only when they were sitting in the back seat of our car. All they heard were news broadcasts, or music.

But sometime in the 1970s, a boutique operation called the Museum of Broadcasting opened in Manhattan. You could actually listen to old radio shows there. I hauled the family to the "museum," which took up two rooms at "Black Rock," the CBS enclave in Midtown.

Several people could listen at once to the same old radio shows. I checked out the catalogue, and requested *Captain Midnight*. My two boys, Mark and Mike, and I plugged in our outsize headsets and waited.

And then we heard the bells intoning midnight. My youngest, Mike, tapped me on my elbow in acknowledgment. When the announcer came on with the words "Captain Midnight," I was exonerated. Their dad had been telling the truth—he had not made up any stories about his own childhood. If *Captain Midnight* were true—why, then, so were all those bizarre tales of playing in the streets of Brooklyn, eluding buses and cars, or of the golden snake that attempted to invade my grandmother's farmhouse, where we spent our summers.

I became so enamored of this little museum that I wrote the first full-length story about it in the *New York Times*. Eventually, it outgrew radio-only and has morphed into the Museum of Television and Radio. But this is how I began my story back in 1977, and as I look at it for the first time in many years, I realize I wasn't only writing about my sons:

> *"Return with us now to those thrilling days of yesteryear. The Lone Ranger rides again."*
>
> Eyes fixed straight ahead to a screen, a 10-year-old boy peers at Ed Sullivan introducing the Beatles "for the first time on any stage in the United States."
>
> A few feet away, a 4-year-old is listening to the finale of the "William Tell" Overture, which heralds the Lone Ranger's arrival. Behind him, two teen-agers are giggling as Ricky Ricardo rushes to the hospital, where Lucy is having a baby.
>
> *"Lux Presents Hollywood!"*
>
> This action takes place at the Museum of Broadcasting, tucked away on the third floor, reached by a narrow elevator, at One East 53d Street, an almost invisible building just a few feet from Paley Park.
>
> . . . *"Again we present the Dental Clinic of the Air"* . . .

My kids loved it.

✳

America grew up with radio once upon a time, and we, its children, were raised on the cereals and other breakfast foods that sponsored the shows: Quaker Oats, Ovaltine, Cheerioats (before its name change), Wheaties, Ralston, Post Toasties.

In all of the United States in 1928, a country of 120 million people, there were 650,000 radios. That was one radio for every 46 households. A year later there were 842,548 sets, and the numbers grew exponentially.

By 1950, as television was insinuating itself, America had an average of two radios per household. I have a *New York Daily News* issue from 1929. It contains a three-quarter-page ad for an Atwater Kent "No. 55" radio with "Dynamic Speaker." The price is $136, not including the tubes—at a time when $35 a week was a livable salary. The Atwater Kent is in a carved cabinet atop four legs. You could get it for $13.60 down, "plus small carrying charge." That hefty radio would be the centerpiece of the living room.

Often, Sunday company stayed around to listen to Winchell and his breathless broadcasts. As soon as he came on the air, someone said "Shh!" and I stopped talking and started listening. I'm not sure my grand-mother—and certainly my almost-deaf grandfather—understood what Winchell was talking about. He spoke quickly and used journalistic lingo, about people in government, or insiders he knew. But there they were, my grandparents, nodding along with my aunts and uncles.

Of course, when President Roosevelt had something to say, Grandma and Grandpa always listened on the radio. Roosevelt had a patrician accent—he was, after all, from a different class from my European-born grandparents—and this made him automatically smart.

"He is some speaker," my grandmother used to say. I don't think she understood much of what he said. He often used arcane expressions, describing our soldiers as being at their "appointed stations," and "we must continue to forge the weapons of victory." But his voice had such depth, and he was, after all, the president, so just hearing his voice made you feel you were part of history. Until he came along, until radio, who in my grandparents' social class had ever heard the head of the country speak?

I believe I was part of the first, or, at the latest, the second, generation to grow up listening to, and being affected by, such strong outside forces. Think about it: For virtually all of recorded history, children learned from parents or schools or books that the schools recommended. To a lesser degree, there were newspapers. Suddenly, as the twentieth century approached its midpoint, a new source of information emerged, bring-ing with it powerful forces. Until then, who ever heard the head of a country, or president or prime minister, speak? Who knew of events happening simultaneously just a few miles away—let alone thousands of miles away? Sure, you found out the next day—if you read the newspapers. But how could uneducated people hear learned professors debating?

These forces, all coming over the radio, shaped to a degree newspapers never could my sense of America, of who I was, of what were the institutions around me, and even of values of good and evil and charity. They also stretched my imagination, my feeling for the spoken word, my sense that there was something bigger out there for me, for all of us.

Until my generation, when rural America still was an overwhelming influence on the American psyche, what radio shows were there for ten-year-olds on the farm to be influenced by? And even if such broadcasts were available, chances are the heavy amount of farm work expected even from youngsters would have precluded listening to radio.

That changed, of course, as the war ended and the world expanded for all of us. So while I was so attentive in Brooklyn, way out in South Dakota another boy, nearly my age, was also listening. I wondered, as I began to write, what it was like for others.

"The 'Fat Man' steps on the scales," recalled Tom Brokaw from his NBC studio. "You know, when you lived on the prairie and you listened to those radio shows, well, you might have been listening to beings from another planet.

"My first memory of radio—I was eight years old, and we were listening to the Joe Louis–Jersey Joe Walcott fight. I was a big Joe Louis fan, and you could tell he was losing the fight. It went fifteen rounds to a decision, and before it was announced, I went to my room and cried. Probably Don Dunphy was doing the radio announcing." Brokaw's memory is pretty good. The fight took place in New York in 1947, and Louis, in the opinion of most observers, was outpointed. But Walcott ran in the final round, presumably thinking he had a big lead and just had to avoid a knockout.

"There's an unwritten rule in boxing that you never take a champion's crown by decision," said Brokaw. "So Louis was declared the winner."

Like me, Brokaw recalls "a big console. I'd do my homework and listen at the same time. We had a wonderful announcer in Sioux City, Iowa, called Whitey Larsen. He'd say, 'Ladies, you can hang out the wash. I think it'll be dry enough tonight.' I later learned that some nights he did the news wearing a band uniform from his local town. The station was 570 on the dial, five thousand watts, but radio waves transmitted extremely well across the plains. It was WNAX—the home station of Lawrence Welk."

We had something else in common, Tom and I: We preferred Roy

Rogers over Gene Autry. "There was always a division between the Autry and Rogers fans," said Brokaw. "My brother was a Gene Autry fan." I don't know why Brokaw preferred Roy, but to me there was something more sparkly about him. He had the great palomino horse, Trigger, and his clothes fit better than Autry's, who was somewhat paunchy. But I digress.

"I remember Ivory Soap, 'it floats,'" said Brokaw. "And I remember my mother listening to Arthur Godfrey. These people were very big deals in our lives—when Arthur Godfrey fired Julius LaRosa, my mother and grandmother gave up on Godfrey. They said he had lost his humility."

That is an interesting recollection, for Godfrey fired LaRosa on the air, explaining later that he felt LaRosa, a boyish singer with a Sinatra-like voice, who had just come out of the Navy, was "losing his humility" and acting too much the star.

Asked about the news announcers, he remembered, Brokaw said, "I heard Lowell Thomas. For years I could do a great Edward R. Murrow imitation." Had he ever met any of his radio heroes? "Yes, I met Bill Shirer and Eric Sevareid."

And what did it do for your imagination? "Imagination was what you had," said Brokaw. "You filled in the screen on the console with those voices. It's the single most intimate medium there is. To this day I have a great place in my life for radio memories."

As I said good-bye to Brokaw, I told him how others I had spoken to had echoed much of what he said.

"I know," he replied. "This is great stuff."

※

As for the urban kids in the time before radio, the forces that shaped them outside the house came from the street. Also, I suspect that even city children in the generation before mine were expected to do their share of housework. So besides mom and dad, and schools (for those children who attended), who or what piqued the imagination? Yes, books, of course. But where did the broader "culture" come from, the sense of being an American, an awareness of the wider world? For ten-year-olds were unlikely to have been avid newspaper readers. But radio—it gave us access to worlds with which our parents were unfamiliar. It wasn't just the children's shows we listened to, but also the news programs and quiz shows, and even the soaps. Yet, I understood the gap between what I was listening to on radio and the three-dimensional world of reality that I inhabited. In other words, I no more would have thought of bopping a bad guy on the head than I would have looked around for a horse to ride on my way to school. I understood the real from the fake, despite my hours spent listening to radio. It did not fool me into believing in the make-believe world, as some social critics and psychologists have charged and continue to believe about television's strong influence. I don't believe watching *Gunsmoke* created a generation of kids looking to out-draw and shoot someone, although its weekly introduction showed a shootout between James Arness and an outlaw. Nor did anyone I ever heard of jump off a building, thinking he could fly, after listening to *Superman*.

Television, though, liberated my hard-of-hearing grandfather—especially when he watched wrestling. Here, he could sit in front of the set and rise and fall with the shenanigans on the screen. As the good guy picked up the bad guy in an airplane spin, my grandfather would raise his legs and then—whomp!—as the bad guy was tossed to the mat, my grandfather's legs would bang the carpet.

But that was in the future.

The politician who mattered to me was Fiorello La Guardia, the mayor. Perhaps it was because I was nine years old, and there was a newspaper strike in New York City. That meant no comic strips. But La Guardia went on the air one Sunday morning and read the "funnies," as we used to call them. He animatedly read "Dick Tracy" in particular, describing the various characters, and ending his description of that day's strip with the admonition, "And so, children, what does that mean? It means that dirty money never brings any luck. . . . dirty money always brings sorrow and sadness and misery and disgrace."

Who could turn to a life of crime after that warning? Why, it was even more sobering than the Shadow's famous "the weed of crime bears bitter fruit. Crime does not pay."

I wasn't the only one listening to the exhortation, not by a long shot. Up in the Bronx, a fellow my age named Colin Powell grew up with radio. We went on to become City College classmates. He took ROTC, became a general, headed the Joint Chiefs of Staff, and eventually got his biggest job—secretary of state.

I wondered what impact radio had on him—could you tell something about the man by what he had listened to years earlier? Would Tom Brokaw have become an inquisitive newsman if he hadn't been imagining the outside world from the South Dakota plains? Would Bill Parcells have become less of a coach without giving his undivided attention to radio in the afternoons?

One day toward the end of Powell's tenure in President George W. Bush's cabinet, I asked the secretary about radio.

"My memory is rapidly fading," Powell said good-naturedly. "But here goes. Unlike movies or TV, radio made you create your own images to fit the words which stretched the imagination." My sentiments exactly. And Brokaw's.

"I remember the Lone Ranger, Amos and Andy, and the Green Hornet," Powell added. "The one most vivid to me is The Shadow: 'Who knows what secrets lurk in the hearts of men? The shadow knows.'"

Interestingly, Powell mistakenly substituted "secrets" for "evil." The Shadow actually said "Who knows what evil lurks in the hearts of men?" Perhaps that slip is not so surprising when you consider that a secretary of state is concerned with both secrets and evil. Thus, he continued, "Also remember those mystery/crime shows with all the footstep sound effects."

Powell had an advantage over me when he listened to his shows in the Bronx. He was joined by his Jamaican-born father.

"My dad used to listen to and heed Gabriel Heatter," explained Powell. "Don't remember listening to much news, but we all knew who Edward R. Murrow was." And Powell also admitted, "I listened to radio while pretending to do homework."

Besides sharing our shows, I discovered one other thing we had in common: the radio itself. "My main radio was an Emerson clock-alarm," he said, "which was a pretty new thing, as I recall. Bakelite—remember that?"

As if I could forget—nor could he.

Chapter 3

Daytime

Radio's great run paralleled almost two decades of crisis in America: the Great Depression followed by World War II. Talk about the need for escapism.

And while my earliest memories are of the 1940s and the daily radio reports about the war, or of watching at our local movie house the weekly newsreels filled with troops landing on foreign shores to the roar of cannons, on the radio serials the good guys always won—but only after a terrible struggle. And usually, there was a lesson in Americanism as well.

So each day, I left my friends and the street games of New York City—punchball, stickball, box baseball (played on the sidewalks)—and came into the house to listen. The radio serials were on two networks—the Mutual Broadcasting System (WOR, 710 on the AM dial) and the American Broadcasting Company (WJZ, 770).

Once tuned in, I stayed with my favorites—few of us switched from one station to the other, even though there were competing broadcasts. At 5:15, for example, WOR was presenting *The Adventures of Superman,* while WJZ aired *Terry and the Pirates.* At 5:30, it was Captain Midnight against Jack Armstrong. In fact, you could separate your friends by the programs they listened to—almost as if you could tell a Yankee fan from a Dodger fan.

Indeed, the distinction between what was on at 710 on the dial, versus the show broadcast at 770, led to one of my young life's low points, a moment I should not be proud of, but somehow take as a badge of honor.

One winter's day I was playing near a metal spiked fence with a friend, who was perhaps a year older. I broke off an icicle that was dangling from a shrub behind the fence.

"Hey, don't do that," he warned, armed with the scientific knowledge of the times. "You'll get sick if you eat an icicle."

Because he was older, I listened. But then I saw another icicle, and I climbed the fence to reach it. I knew he was looking, so I made believe I simply was scaling the fence and tried to hide the icicle in my right hand, while I held on to the top of the fence with my left between the spikes. But the metal was icy. I slipped—and impaled myself on the fence.

I pulled myself off and headed home, afraid to tell anyone what happened. There was a hole in the right side of my stomach. I would wait for my mother to get home from work. When she arrived, I told her what had happened. Immediately, she got my Uncle Sol, a bookmaker who usually was home during the afternoon, to drive me to Kings County Hospital. He was the only one we knew who had a car.

At the hospital, they put me in a room with four other children who had just undergone appendicitis operations. Luckily for me, I didn't require surgery. There was one radio in the room. The next afternoon, at 5:15, I wanted to listen to *Superman* on WOR. But the kids in the other beds demanded *Terry and the Pirates* on WJZ. They won. I was, after all, the new kid in the ward.

Frustrated, but mobile, unlike my antagonists, who were stitched up, I stood up in my bed and urinated on the boys in the beds on either side of me. They screamed and cried but were helpless. This was, indeed, like a feud between Yankees fans and Dodgers fans. Luckily for me, these other kids had stitches in their sides, and the railings on the bed kept them from getting out. They couldn't get to me. But when I left the hospital the next day, they all serenaded me with, "We hate to see you go . . ." and tacked on the classic Brooklyn ending, ". . . We hope to heck you never come back, we hate to see you go."

Decades later, I told this story to my children as part of their nightly bedtime tuck-in tales. They were, of course, fascinated, and I soon learned that every mishap of my childhood was fodder for their goodnight stories. Were they enamored of the fact that a child had done something naughty? Or was it simply that their old man, who like every parent preached right from wrong, was hardly perfect?

I'm not exactly sure. But I'll say this: as I sat down to write this book,

I told my youngest, Mike, what I had planned to do, and he said to me, "Don't forget to tell them the hospital story."

"What's that?" I asked.

"Remember—when you urinated on the other kids?" Of course; how could I have forgotten that? Ah, what we did for our radio shows.

Chapter 4

Playing Hooky

I always took an extra day to recover from childhood ills such as whooping cough or the croup or measles because of the daytime cliff-hangers. Yes, when you were home from school during the week, and saddled with a fever of 102, there was nothing else to do but listen to day-time radio.

And so, while my heart was with those children's adventure shows, they didn't appear until the early evening hours. I had to listen to something in the morning and afternoons. Thus, the daytime soaps became a part of my life, too. Even now, I mention a soap to my wife and she responds with the name of the heroine, or sponsor, or the time of day it was on.

For me, the show that mattered most was *Queen for a Day*. Talk about radio inextricably knotted with your own life—I devised ways I could get my mother on that show and make life easier for her. In a time when divorce was never spoken of—indeed, in New York State back then, adultery virtually was the only permitted reason to divorce—my mother was a divorcée.

Women who were contestants on radio either were identified as being married or single or widowed. I remember my confusion when my mother and I attended a radio show called *Quick as a Flash*. Members from the audience were invited to be on a panel to try to solve a murder mystery.

Before the broadcast, the announcer asked if there were any single women who wanted to go up. I nudged my mother to raise her hand, but she kept it down. Then they asked if there were any married women who wanted to go on the show. This was more problematic for me. She was a mother, yes, but she wasn't married. Still, I asked her to put up her hand. She declined.

At that moment I understood that I stood on confused ground: my mother wasn't married, and she was single with a child. Yet, she had been married. So where did this put her? Where did I fit into this setting? Where did I fit in, period?

It was a question I struggled with for much of my pre-teen and teenage years, never coming to a resolution. Yet, today, it's a question hardly asked of children, or parents. Single parent. Two parents. Same-sex parents. Adoptive parents. The other day, I went to a park in Greenwich Village with my older grandson, Corey. The sign on the gate read, "Children and guardians only." As if using the word "parent" would insult those youngsters (and guardians, or nannies, or babysitters) who were there without a mother or father.

Yet, here I was listening to *Queen for a Day,* with the ebullient Jack Bailey opening the broadcast by shouting, "Do you want to be queen for a day?" and ending his show with the hopeful words, ". . . hoping I can make every woman in America—Queen for every Day!" I thought: how many days in a year, and how long would it take all those tens of millions of women to become Queen for a Day? Would my mother's own day ever come?

The show's premise was arresting, and maudlin: usually a woman (always a mother) was struggling along without a basic necessity to make life's work easier—a washing machine (for her eight children's clothes); a pretty dress (to wear to her daughter's graduation), a vacuum cleaner (to clean up her handicapped child's room). There were four "contestants"—women who had the weight of the world on their shoulders. Bailey, a former carnival barker who sported a thin mustache and slicked-back hair that started V-shaped over his forehead, was nevertheless respectful of the poor souls who made it to the microphone. Later, when he went on television, *TV Guide* would describe him as the "Number One mesmerizer of middle-aged females and most relentless dispenser of free washing machines."

The women's stories were told—and then the audience voted. The winner, who received the loudest applause according to an "applause meter," got her surprise that would alter her life, along with a host of other gifts. But even though I was twelve when I first heard the program, something about it seemed odd to me: the mothers were chosen from the audience, yet at the end of the program, Bailey announced a very specific prize to be awarded—say a Whirlpool washing machine, or a farm tractor.

I soon wondered whether this was fixed—or perhaps his crack staff had started to man the phones as soon as contestants came out of the audience, and the people behind the scenes were calling various stores to find out whether they carried the product that would change this dear woman's life. When, finally, she was crowned, the orchestra played "Pomp and Circumstance."

Who could be more deserving than my own mother? She trudged off to work each day—the only mother in the neighborhood who did. She came home after six o'clock. She often worked Saturdays. Yet, she also made sure when she was free to take me into Manhattan, to take me to Macy's, or the Gilbert Hall of Science (which sold microscopes and telescopes and chemistry sets) in the Flatiron Building, or to watch a parade, or to row a boat in Brooklyn's Prospect Park. But I also knew it wasn't to be—divorced women would not be going on the radio, no matter how deserving. Instead, someone from far away—never a New Yorker—would be crowned, and would get a torrent of gifts that would magically transform her life.

I suppose I always had this magical thinking. Perhaps the radio shows ingrained this into me, or at least offered the possibility that magic was viable in my life. There were two night-time programs that I thought might be able to change my mother's life, which for me meant her having a husband, even if it meant getting back together again with my father. One of the broadcasts was called *Alexander's Mediation Board*, and was presided over by Dr. A. L. Alexander. Back then, middle initials, or initials of any sort, conferred status on the speaker. The theme of Dr. Alexander's show was, "There are two sides to every story." The other family-problem-solving show was *The Good Will Hour*, with John J. Anthony listening to real-life problems and then rendering his opinion. He had twenty million listeners, who heard a spouse begin her plea to him with, "Mr. Anthony, I have a problem." Comedians took to calling him "Mr. Agony." My father told me he tried to get on the show in an attempt to iron out things with my mother, but they didn't choose him.

One day in the early 1950s, my uncle told me a friend of his was coming over to our house. My uncle had to step out for a while, so I was to greet the friend. He came in, and I asked him to sit in the living room. I was barely into my teens, and probably was not a great host. The friend was pleasant, and reserved. We had a banal conversation, and soon my uncle returned. Later that night, my uncle told me that the friend was the son of John J. Anthony. "But he doesn't talk to his father," explained my uncle. "His parents are divorced."

So the great John J. Anthony was unable to solve his own family troubles. I'm glad he didn't try to solve mine.

Later, when I grew old enough to think about working and adulthood, I always imagined that with my first paycheck I'd send my mother a dozen roses. I pictured her smiling, with tears coming down her cheeks— just as I imagined the winner on *Queen for a Day,* as she was showered with gifts, had a tiara put on her head, and was handed a rose.

But I never did that for my mother. I never sent her on a cruise to Europe or bought her a mink or did any of the things I always promised myself I would do one day. And then one day she died.

All those dreams I had for her never came true. And of course, life for her was no radio show with a finite daily (happy) ending. It was a series of struggles, and instead of my grandiose dreams, I should have done the little things instead. Like sending only one rose, once in a while. Yet, my mother never, ever asked for anything or even expressed dismay with the apparent difficulties she faced.

We often listened to grown-up radio together. That's how I learned about Hollywood and Broadway and show-business myths. It's how I learned about politics, and the 1930s, and the quirky side of life. Indeed, my mother was the type who laughed at pratfall jokes—you know, someone slipping on a banana peel.

Thus I learned about Jean Harlow and her mysterious death, or whether Barbara Stanwyck was overacting in *Sorry, Wrong Number* on Lux Radio Theatre, or that Vivien Leigh had a voice coach to learn to affect a Southern accent for *Gone With the Wind.* And I appreciated the zany humor of the Marx Brothers, where the banana peel was part of their world.

But we never listened together during the day. She was working; I might have been home on some excuse. So after she left, I started my radio day by listening to *Breakfast with Dorothy and Dick, The Fitzgerald's,* and *Tex and Jinx.*

Dorothy was Dorothy Kilgallen; Dick was Richard Kollmar. Each morning the couple broadcast from a place the announcer described as their "Park Avenue apartment." You could hear them talking to their butler,

Julius, who brought them coffee. I could hear their bird whistling in the background.

She used to call him "Sweetie," and invariably the morning began with a recitation of the previous night's doings in Café Society. They visited their haunts: the Stork Club, or El Morocco, or they took in a Broadway show, or dined at some fabulous restaurant. What a perfect couple, but lampooned mercilessly (and fictitiously) in Woody Allen's *Radio Days*. But she was a journalist—in the full-sized, but tabloidy, *New York Journal-American*, and I already was fascinated with newspaper people. He was a nationally known radio personality playing the role of "Boston Blackie," a wise-cracking, tough-talking private eye.

I listened to them before Dorothy had become a staple on the Sunday night television show *What's My Line?* and whose somewhat smarmy style and mousy smile made her an object of derision for many viewers. After all, she examined the inside labels of men's suits to see if the guest was wearing something expensive, and she cleverly figured out many occupations. She was part of a panel that usually included the actress Arlene Francis and Random House publisher Bennett Cerf. The panel had twenty questions to guess the "line," or occupation, of the guest. Each "no" answer brought the guest five dollars. But there was a maximum of ten "no's," or fifty dollars. We got excited at home over that.

On the radio, though, Ms. Kilgallen was having breakfast in her sixteen-room apartment, talking things over with her "hubby" and enriching my stay-at-home mornings with another take on the perfect home life. They often brought their children to the microphone as well, and this combination of hearth and sophisticated night-life chatter made me imagine how wonderful newspapering could be.

So she died of an overdose mixture, and conspiracy theorists believed she was part of that interconnected web of Kennedy-assassination insiders who knew too much and were conveniently found dead. The conspiracy theorists believed this because once she had bragged that she would break open the Kennedy assassination story, implying she had some inside information. Forget about the fact that her husband was home (asleep in another room) and so was one of her children, when she died. Her name appears forever in Web sites devoted to the "Who Really Killed Kennedy?" cults.

In any event, another of my fantasy family people succumbed in a not very pretty way.

Dorothy and Dick were part of the morning threesome of talky husband-and-wife teams: with the Fitzgeralds and Tex and Jinx, the three were on contiguous stations on the dial. But Dorothy was the newsperson; hence, my fascination.

When the husband-and-wife teams put down their morning coffee and went on to their daily business, there was a lull for me until the soaps came on after lunch. Oh, there was the Arthur Godfrey show, with its roster of singers and the folksy host, as well as *The Breakfast Club,* and news programs, and music. But the serious business of family drama was yet a few hours away.

The Fitzgeralds—Ed and Pegeen—also broadcast out of their apartment. He was a clever, somewhat cynical, self-made and interesting guy—no formal education, knocked around as an actor, joined the Royal Air Force during World War I. She was a small-town girl with liberal views. He quoted Shakespeare. They had no children, but seemed to have a full life with a host of friends. They made you want to live in Manhattan.

Tex and Jinx, on the other hand, had a softer edge, perhaps because of his Southwest accent. He was actually a high-powered publicist for the Republican party, and coined the slogan "I Like Ike" after convincing Eisenhower to run for president. She had been one of the country's most famous models at the dawn of the 1940s, and had a minor film career. Their show was more about interviewing others than about themselves. She was a sort of gee-whiz, aren't-you-nice interviewer, while he was issues-oriented. Unlike the glamorous life led by Dorothy and Dick, or the homespun adventures of Ed and Pegeen, Tex and Jinx was perhaps the first major interview show. If you listened, you became smarter.

The Fitzgeralds left the air at 9 a.m., when *The Breakfast Club,* with Don McNeill, came on. It was broadcast in Chicago from the Parker House, which was another symbol to me of an America I longed to be part of. I knew of Parker House from the Automat—it featured Parker House rolls. And when I realized that the show I was listening to had a connection with those buttery little twists I ate in the Automat, well, it was too perfect. It was a way to become one with America, and apple pie, and even . . . yes, I'll say it . . . . a glazed ham. The kind criss-crossed with slash marks, dotted with cloves, golden-brown from the oven. The kind I used to see in my mother's *Ladies Home Journal.* But certainly never in my mother's kitchen.

"Don McNeill wanted to make a neighborhood of a nation," a chronicler of the show, John Doolittle, once wrote. McNeill went into his audience and spoke to people who had shown up from all over the United States. I would listen to many of these small-town folks making small talk with the host, who also had celebrities drop in—Groucho Marx, for one, even artist Norman Rockwell.

Each segment began with a "call to breakfast," as if it were a diner on a train, or the lobby of a great hotel. There was a "first call to breakfast," and forty-five minutes later a "fourth call to breakfast—Philco call to breakfast!" Philco made radios, later television sets, and was as noted in the forties as Sony is today. Another sponsor was Swift, which turned out millions of tins of ham—another slice of the American pie, so to speak, forbidden to me. But while the food, and even the characters, were alien, the show had a beguiling quality, even to a boy in Brooklyn.

There was a band and a character named Aunt Fanny. She was actually Fran Allison, whom I came to appreciate again years later when she appeared on TV as the middle, real-life member of *Kukla, Fran and Ollie*. But her Aunt Fanny persona was typical of the humor of those days—an addled farm lady talking about her friends named Bert and Bertie, or the Smelsers, or Ott Ort. She was reminiscent of the Minnie Pearl character on *Grand Ole Opry* of Saturday nights, where Minnie would show up in her store-bought hat (which still had a label dangling from it) and shout "How-dee!" to raucous applause. Indeed, photos of Fran Allison depicted her wearing hand-me-down or homemade dresses and silly feathered hats. That farm quality I see now actually was a mid-America sensibility. Thus, McNeill often had prayer sessions on the show and no one in broadcasting thought that was odd. His humor? "Courtship makes a man spoon; marriage makes him fork over." The audience loved it. I loved it.

"Don't forget Don McNeill and his gang saying 'so long, and be good to your neighbor'" was the way he ended each show. Each one began with the sprightly song:

Good morning, breakfast-clubbers, Good morning to ya,
We got up bright and early to howdy-do-ya!

The show lasted thirty-five years, longer than any other show in radio history.

Godfrey, meanwhile, had a "family" on air: He was the head, and there was the basso announcer Tony Marvin, Archie Bleyer, the bandleader, and singers whom Godfrey bantered with. I wound up having a connection (tenuous, I'll admit) to Godfrey, who, in his time, was the biggest star of radio, and then on television. Back in 1953, as a junior at Thomas Jefferson High School in Brooklyn, I sat in front of a bored, wisecracking guy named Sidney Leibowitz. We were in an English class. He was always joking with friends in the other rows; I don't think he thought about Hemingway much.

One day, the teacher, exasperated at the noise always coming from his end of the room, blurted out, "Will you please stop talking, Leibowitz, or Lawrence, or whatever your name is!" For Sidney had recently appeared on the *Arthur Godfrey Talent Scouts* show, taking the names of two nephews, Steve and Lawrence. As Steve Lawrence, he got the highest score on the applause meter and was the night's winner—starting a singing career that went on for another fifty years or so with his wife, Eydie Gorme.

But he was still in high school then. And so, like the rest of us, he had to take tests. During one literature exam, he poked me in the back and whispered, "Put your paper on the right side so I can see it." I did. My claim to fame? Steve Lawrence copied off me—and failed an English test.

Godfrey and McNeill, Ed and Pegeen, Tex and Jinx, Dorothy and Dick—they took up the mornings. But they hardly were alone. This is my selective recollection (aided by a vintage newspaper's radio page) of what early morning programming was available when I was in my radio prime, Friday, April 2, 1948:

5:45 AM— WOR—News of the Farm
6:00 AM— WJZ—Farm News
        WCBS—Arthur Godfrey Variety Show
        WHN—Newsreel Theatre
        WNEW—Anything Goes (variety)
6:30 AM— WOR—Rambling with Gambling
        WINS—Farm news
7:00 AM— WNBC—News; Bob Smith show
        WJZ—News; Don Gardiner
        WOR—News; Melvin Elliott
7:15 AM— WOR—Gambling's Musical Clock
7:55 AM— WNYC, News, weather; Help Wanted
8:05 AM— WQXR—Morning Symphony
8:15 AM— WOR—Breakfast with Dorothy and Dick

WJZ—Ed and Pegeen Fitzgerald
WNYC—Consumers Guide
8:30 AM— WNYC—Hi Jinx [later to become "Tex and Jinx"]
8:55 AM— WHN—News; Carlton Fredericks
9:00 AM— WJZ—The Breakfast Club
WMCA—the Duke Ellington Show
9:05 AM— WQXR—Piano Personalities
9:15 AM— WOR—the Passing Parade
10 AM— WCBS—Missus Goes A-Shopping
WMCA—News; Tommy Dorsey
WINS—Listen to Lacy
WHN—Ted Husing's Bandstand
WNEW—Make Believe Ballroom

At the bottom of the page was a one-column short labeled "TELEVI-SION." It took up three lines. They included WCBS-TV, which from 11 a.m. to 5 p.m. was broadcasting a test pattern—that's right, six hours of nothing but the CBS logo.

As for dominant radio, it was obvious that competing programmers sensed they had to fight fire with fire—not against television, but against rival radio stations. So there were those dueling husband-and-wife talks shows at breakfast-time, and then, at ten in the morning, battling bands—from Tommy Dorsey to disk jockeys on *Listen to Lacy,* Ted Husing's *Bandstand,* and *Make Believe Ballroom* (hosted by Martin Block, a celebrity disk jockey).

Make Believe Ballroom was the musical show that mattered most for us, especially on Saturday mornings. For that was the only time we really could listen to it legally (I mean, if we didn't play hooky). Strictly speaking, it wasn't a show—rather a compendium of the week's top-selling popular records.

It had a dramatic quality for us—would the song "It's Magic" move up "three buttons" (from fourth to first) to replace "Buttons and Bows"? What did we know of payola, if in fact there was something suspicious about these best-sellers? It was important to us to know what the biggest hits were. So each week, Block would begin his countdown to Number One, and say a little something about each record, and whether it was the first time on the list, or had fallen or moved down in national sales.

Thus, early in our teens we learned about "That Singing Rage, Miss

Patti Page," who sang of her lost love in "Tennessee Waltz." We discovered new singing groups such as the Four Lads, the Four Tops, the Four Aces, the Four Preps, the Four Coins, the Four Freshmen, the Four Knights. Not to mention Eileen Barton ("If I Knew You Were Coming I'd've Baked a Cake"), or perky Teresa Brewer ("Till I Waltz Again With You"). What they all had were mellow voices with a distinctive sound. They could go it alone, without being drowned out by electrified music. Their solo hits on a record lasted fewer than three minutes—hard to believe you'd fork over money to hear one song. Of course, there was another song on the other side of the disk, but usually that was considered a throw-in.

So late Saturday mornings, I'd be next to the radio, rooting for my favorite record to move up, if not all the way to Number One. Who made these decisions on which was Number One? We never questioned the methodology. This was like an athletic contest, and when it was over we'd all meet in the street to discuss or argue over the results. When people today talk of the 1940s and 1950s being a "simpler time," it implies the era was not so passionate. It was. It just wasn't as strident as today, with its reality-based programming or its plethora of in-your-face talk and cable and news shows.

The reality is that there is nothing real about being on television— once the camera is on you, you hardly are acting as you would normally. All those castaways and apprentices and would-be brides know the camera is rolling, and what they say and how they act is as far removed from reality as the Partridge family. Why, even the boardroom that Donald Trump presides over to "fire" his aspiring capitalists actually is a stage set. I recall sitting on a charter flight with the New York Jets football team, and talking with the club's play-by-play announcer, Marty Glickman. I was telling him about a football book I was writing. Marty spoke quietly, in his usual off-air demeanor. Then I asked him whether we could talk, on the record, about his experiences. "Sure," he said. I hauled out a tape recorder, put it in front of his lips, and instantly, he shouted into the microphone, "JERRY, I'M GLAD YOU ASKED THAT QUESTION!" And he was off and running. The microphone had created a new reality.

So what was this simpler time? Well, it was a time when you'd hear the "Star Spangled Banner" played when a radio station closed down for the night, usually around midnight. That's right, many stations did not stay on through the night, but simply said good-bye until the morning. And when they came back on the air, they'd do it with the "Star Spangled Banner" again.

And the music—those top-ten or top-twenty records? Sure, they were mushier than today's, no one railing against the machine or president or welfare or fascism. No beating up of "ho's" or "bitches." The singers didn't wear metallic bras or sport tattoos. They merely sang songs, something under three minutes of intelligible words, often corny, never raunchy.

When Johnnie Ray sang "Walkin' My Baby Back Home" and wailed, "We start in to pet/ and that's when I get/her powder all over my vest," it didn't get any more graphic than that. Indeed, the word "pet" did not connote stroking body parts or foreplay, merely touching. Yes, I guess that was simpler. But we didn't see ourselves as living in some "Hairspray" retro age. In fact, what generation ever did see itself as living in a simpler time? It was the most modern time possible, but with imagination still a significant part of our life.

Thus, radio was twinned with music, with dating, with family. What I thought, what I imagined love was, what I thought the outside world was all about—it was tied up, inevitably and inextricably, with radio. Yes, we were already in the jet age—I had gone to an air show when Idlewild International Airport opened after the war and all of us ooh'd and ah'd when the announcer said a jet plane was breaking the sound barrier, and we heard a sonic boom. But Eisenhower still was a radio president. The Korean War was a radio war. You rarely saw an American prisoner of war. Television was coming, but movie stars were more likely to appear on radio shows than on the tube. There was no place on television for a *Make Believe Ballroom*, where the top twenty records could be played— if it were on television, would you be staring at an image of a black 78 r.p.m. disk while Frankie Laine sang "Mule Train"? The idea of a Dick Clark with his daily high school group of teenagers dancing to the day's hit records probably seemed like an absurd idea. And how could you show "The Shadow," an invisible being, on television? When people talk these days about that "simpler time" it denigrates the era, in a way. As if there were no neuroses. As if psychologists and parents didn't concern themselves with violence on the radio. Many of the shows weren't graphic in the sense of being visual; they were graphic if imagination mattered. Our music didn't concern itself with whom we woke up with in the morning—it was more on the order of, can I get a goodnight kiss? That might seem so simple today. Believe me, it was the biggest thing in your life back then.

Radio was flooded with dramas that pricked the imagination, and music that, increasingly in the dawn of the fifties, bothered parents. But we had no outrageous talk shows, no foul-mouthed (of course, in the ear of the beholder) shock-jocks, and never, ever bad language. No "damn" ever passed the lips of Tex or Jinx, or Lamont Cranston, or even the most evil evil-doer on *Captain Midnight* or *Superman.* No one ever was raped on radio, or in music that was aired on radio. Even Cole Porter's "Love for Sale" was banned on the air. As for the more sensual, suggestive recordings by black singers—I'm not talking about Nat King Cole or Dinah Washington, who crossed over into the mainstream—that was relegated to the genre of "race music." Essentially, this was black music that the mainstream radio would not air, but which instead surfaced on radio stations somewhere way up the dial. I sometimes would tune in a station high up, such as WLIB—the call letters standing, of course, for "liberty." I was nineteen years old, still part of a world that was segregated in the arts to a large degree. I heard a screaming voice utter the words "Bo Diddley," and I stopped turning the dial to listen. It had a frenetic sound, but it also had a swift, patterned beat. It was beyond Alan Freed's rock 'n' roll. It was a beat I had not experienced before. But in addition to being noisy, the song also had a tune, not so alien to my youthful sense of tonality. Enthralled, I listened to the record to the end. It was the first time I recall actually listening to—and hearing—what was on a black station. I went out and bought the record. Not that I had a phonograph on which to play it. I just wanted to possess it. My friend Lenny Davis actually owned a phonograph, and I was able to play the disk on his machine.

As I was hitting my teen years, this became known as rhythm and blues, or rock 'n' roll, and often white singers "covered" these records with a less strident, or more mellow sound. (Think Pat Boone singing a slowed-down version of Fats Domino's "Ain't That a Shame," sounding like a high school kid woodenly reading poetry in iambic pentameter for the first time.) The advent of rock 'n' roll signaled the beginning of the loss of innocence in the mind of the next generation. More apocalyptic signs followed with "Rock Around The Clock," as Bill Haley and the Comets told us teenagers in 1954 that we would stay up all night. Doing what? I wondered. The next year it was the soundtrack for the major movie, *The Blackboard Jungle,* about juveniles running wild, and the song took on an aura of godlessness and anti-societal doings. The opening sound track took my breath away—"One, two, three o'clock, four o'clock—Rock!" But the film was the first I recall in which a white guy, the Vic Morrow character, calls the black guy, played by Sidney Poitier, a racial epithet. Poitier portrayed a teenager of fortitude and character, traits not often attributed in the fifties to a black man or woman in movies. I wondered how come I had never seen anything like this before.

Yet, it was not so strange when I think about it. The only occasions on radio an ethnic character was introduced was to evince laughter, or, in the case of a drama, some sinister motive. Similarly, what I knew of the character of other countries often evolved from how foreigners were depicted on the radio. For a person's foreign accent was an easy substitute for character on the air. On kids' shows, my shows, the *Superman* baddies often had easily identifiable German—and then, in the Cold War, Russian—accents. As did the dastards on *Captain Midnight.* A Spanish accent, especially from someone playing a Mexican, connoted a mañana mentality and was a staple on programs such as Jack Benny's. On Fred Allen's *Allen's Alley* there was the convergence of iconic accents: Mrs. Nussbaum's Yiddish; Senator Claghorn's Southern, and Ajax Cassidy's Irish.

Stereotypes helped make the shows easier to digest for children, for me—let's face it, for grown-ups, as well. Bad guys spoke like—well, like people with a thick Brooklyn accent, or someone from a mysterious (and detestable) foreign country. If someone was Italian, he didn't merely have an Italian name. He had a ludicrous Italian accent. Thus, the titled character in *Life With Luigi* said things like "I'm-a-gonna-call-a my momma in Naples." He was described by the narrator as "the little immigrant."

Luigi was played by J. Carrol Naish, in reality a man of Irish descent. Each show began with Luigi writing to his mother back home in Italy, telling her of America's wonders. He was determined to become a citizen and dutifully attended a class each week taught by Miss Spaulding, with other ethnics on hand—Schultz, the German; Olsen, the Scandinavian; Horowitz, the European Jew. Luigi's landlord, Pasquale, had one constant: he tried mightily each week to unload his daughter, Rosa, on Luigi. Rosa was described as plumpish, and whenever she heard her name, she'd come in giggling and say, "You call me, Papa?" Poor Luigi sighed.

The Irish had to be policemen or crime-fighting sidekicks, such as Mike Clancy, who worked for "Mr. Keen," and Sergeant O'Hara, who helped out "The Fat Man," while Mullins was the aide-de-camp of Mr. and Mrs. North. If a French character was introduced, he'd be either a smooth-as-silk lover or a nasally, high-strung dilettante. Of course, the British either were stuffy servants or titled figures. There was one noted show about Jews—*The Goldbergs*—and they were presented in a real-life, middle-class, tenement-living way, with, of course, wise old Uncle Jake.

On other shows, though, Jews were laughable characters: "Mr. Kitzel" on Jack Benny's show, purveying a hot dog and always adding, "with a pickle in the middle and the mustard on top." Or there was the ludicrously named (but funny) Pansy Nussbaum on the Fred Allen show. She was part of a repertory group of characters on his *Allen's Alley*. He would knock on the door of each house, and various oddballs would emerge. Pansy Nussbaum would come out, Allen would say, "Ah, Mrs. Nussbaum," and she would reply, with a Yiddish inflection, "You were expecting maybe Lauren Bagel?" While Russians may have been evil on the children's serials, they were comical on shows such as *Eddie Cantor*, where a fellow named Bert Gordon portrayed a character known as "the mad Russian." On Sunday mornings there was "The Jewish Caravan of Stars," which featured the harmonizing Barry Sisters, who began in the Yiddish theater under their real name as the Bagelman Sisters.

And speaking of sisters: What I knew of women—outside of my mother and grandmother—I knew from radio. Just like a creaky voice on radio dramas signified advanced age in a man, a sultry voice indicated sexiness in a woman. If you didn't know just what type of woman you were listening to, why, the announcers would tell us. One of my favorite shows was *Mr. Keen, Tracer of Lost Persons* (the show's theme song was "Somewhere I'll Find You," and it aired on Thursday nights from 7:30 to 8 "Eastern War Time"). The announcer would introduce the scene by describing Mr. Keen in his office with "his spinster secretary, Miss Alice."

And black characters on radio? They either were laughable, or wise—rarely anything in between. There were no professionals or pals of the white heroes, or even black actors portraying nonblack characters. So we had the lazy "Lightning" of *Amos 'n' Andy*, or the parade of housekeepers, and, occasionally, a warm character named "Beulah," who originally was played by a white male actor. Eventually, the character morphed into Hattie McDaniel, a real black woman (!), and then it carried over to television, where Ethel Waters became the first African American lead character on a sit-com show.

What impact on me did all these black, Irish, and other ethnic characters have? They force-fed a stereotype—OK, a prejudice—of people, how they were slotted. I'm sure that if I had ever met anyone with a British accent before I was, say, twelve years old, I would have thought he or she was a member of the Royal Family—if not a servant of theirs.

These stereotypes were further impressed on me at home—perhaps they even began there, then were given the seal of approval by radio—where people of other ethnic backgrounds were referred to strictly by their religion, or color, or country of origin. Thus, the woman with an accent who worked in a store was a Pollack, because she had come from Poland. When my grandmother mentioned "the Pollack," I knew she was talking about Mary. When my grandmother talked about the "schwartze," Yiddish for a black person, we were talking about the "cleaning girl" who came in once a week. The "Italanya" might have been the guy who delivered ice.

After the war, when Jews who managed to escape the Holocaust arrived in huge numbers, they became known as "refs," or refugees, and "greena's," for "greenhorns." It was funny to me that my grandparents, both of whom had "Jewish" accents, referred to a newcomer as a "greenhorn." As on radio, the stereotypes were not mean-spirited. It was simply a shorthand way of looking at people—by people who never really got to know someone from a different background. So we'd laugh at these exchanges:

Mrs. Nussbaum had trouble with English syntax: "I'm with you speaking," she'd say. Or, Allen would compliment her on a corsage she was wearing: "What are they?" he asked. "Lilies of the alley," she replied.

Ajax Cassidy of Allen's Alley has a black eye and Allen asks him where he got it. Cassidy explains he went to a wedding the day before, and even though it was breakfast, he said to someone, "I'll have a little punch." And, of course, that's how he got the black eye. That show prompted an outpouring of letters from the outraged Irish-American community, which constantly was after Allen to tone down or cut out the drinking and brawling aspect of Cassidy's character.

Senator Claghorn, who also lived in the alley, was a combination of bombastic politician and a Southerner who had an aversion to anything north of the Mason-Dixon Line. Why, Beauregard Claghorn refused water from a Dixie cup. He would not drive through the Lincoln Tunnel. And he would never wear a Union suit (those old fashioned one-piece undergarments always worn around the house by comic farm types).

A foreign accent evoked laughter on comedy shows. What did I know of Brazil? It produced Carmen Miranda, who had a thick accent, was known as "The Brazilian Bombshell," and whose movie persona was that of an emotional dame who sang songs while wearing a foot-high hat filled with tropical fruit. When I visited Rio many years later and mentioned how Carmen Miranda had been my first introduction to the country, people rolled their eyes. She was, to us in the United States, Brazil's most famous personage. But her persona was an embarrassment to many Brazilians. They thought she made Brazil seem like a comic-opera country. In fact, Carmen Miranda was not only the iconic image many Americans had of Brazilian women but also their lasting image of a *Latina* in general. She sang of the "Souse American Way," and when she spoke in mangled English—why, the audience laughed.

I think of how I viewed Carmen Miranda, or Senator Claghorn, or even Luigi, who wanted so much to be Americanized, and see now that back in the 1940s and early 1950s the vistas in my neighborhood were essentially closed to the outside world. For no one in my family—not even my neighbors or the kids I ran around with—had a friend who wasn't from the same ethnic background. And the same economic level. Only on the most cursory level did I ever speak to or come in contact with a non-Jew—and certainly not to discuss anything vaguely intimate such as the Dodgers or the weather. I, and everyone I knew, grew up without once socializing with a black person.

✳

Late at night, just into my teen years, I discovered a new type of show—all-night talk radio. I began listening to a character named Long John Nebel, who described himself as a former carnival barker. He claimed his father actually coined the name "Baby Ruth" for the chocolate bar, while working for the Curtiss Candy Company, so that it didn't have to pay the real Babe Ruth any royalties. Curtiss had always claimed that its candy bar was named for President Grover Cleveland's daughter, who was America's darling at the turn of the twentieth century. But this would be a typical Nebel contention, with what seemed a nugget of truth in there somewhere. He hit it big in radio when he started interviewing a string of nutcases, or out-and-out frauds, who claimed to have been on space ships. Long John even had a guest who brought in a record of Venutian music. Another guy, named Howard Menger, told Nebel a flying saucer landed in his apple orchard in New Jersey, while a fellow named George Adamski talked of being visited by people from Venus.

This was in the early 1950s, and I knew the damn stuff was ridiculous. But one night, after Nebel claimed there were alien sightings near the station's radio transmitter in Cartaret, New Jersey, I called my friend Don Eremin. Like me, Don often had trouble sleeping as we figured out what to do with our lives, and we hopped into his car and drove at three in the morning to Cartaret. We were looking for flashing lights or a humming noise or anything that could be construed as emanating from something constructed outside our planet. I actually went to the transmitter, which contained a shack and one lonely fellow. I asked him about flying saucers and he had no idea what I was talking about. Seems he didn't even listen to the show that was being beamed above him. As Don and I drove back to Brooklyn, we wondered whether Nebel had been making the stuff up.

My teenage insomnia was softened by my ability to listen to these late-night personalities. I discovered Barry Gray, and Joe Franklin, and Jean Shepherd, along with Long John. Of course, I had the radio tuned to whisper level, which made it hard to hear. It's easier to listen to soft music than to hear people speaking on a radio turned quite low.

Shepherd was perfect for a teenager getting to know the world and just becoming aware of its foibles. Maybe even a bit rebellious, too. He made fun of big business and serious politicians. There was something conspiratorial about the relationship he had with his listeners, and I found him delightfully subversive. He once was in contact with a listener in a car who actually had a car phone (remember, this was the fifties), and suggested the man drive through a toll booth without paying. Live, on the air, we heard the man exclaim as he drove through—"I didn't pay!" Shepherd also would ask his listeners to kick on their bright lights (the high-beam button was on the floor, next to the brake) as they drove to acknowledge they were part of the broadcast audience.

Another somewhat subversive act was to tell us to lower the radio, and then put it on the window sill. Then he'd ask us to open the window. He then administered the coup de grace. "Turn up the volume," he said softly. And when we did, a moment later he'd start to scream into the microphone, which must have scared the hell out of my neighbors, as well as confusing them. For they didn't recognize the voice. Some weirdo was shouting from the second floor at 843 Sutter Avenue.

Although this was only a few years removed from radio's heyday, Shepherd bathed us in nostalgia with his talk of secret-decoder badges, whistling rings, a Daisy rifle, and Christmas plum pudding—the closest I ever got to the latter was in a Dickens story. Shepherd spoke of his father, a guy overwhelmed by the modernity of the 1930s. His father, Jean said, was convinced the government had a pill that turned water into gasoline. But the government was keeping it from us in order not to destroy the big oil companies.

That father was portrayed in *A Christmas Story,* the wonderful movie based on Shepherd's short stories of growing up. Shepherd liked to claim that none of the stories actually happened to him, but his memory must have been playing tricks. I'm sure he had a set of Lionel trains, as well as all the other fantasy toys of a Depression-era child.

When I got to City College of New York and became somewhat of a big shot as editor of the school paper, I had a terrific idea. C.C.N.Y. was a school without tuition that we proud poor kids thought of as the Harvard of the proletariat. We had a great soccer team, made better, I'm sure, because half the players were immigrants—that is, they came from soccer-playing countries. We had a game coming up against West Point, and I thought, this is something that might appeal to Shepherd: poor kids from the sidewalks of New York playing Army wannabes. Maybe he'd like to give us a pep talk? I called the station cold, and his producer put Shepherd on the air. "Sounds great," he said. "When do you want to do it?"

I organized an outdoor rally on the campus lawn and Shepherd showed up in front of a thousand kids, and made a speech describing this venture as "a bunch of students from City College playing some bullet-headed cadets whose fathers knew Congressmen." The City students loved it, and Shepherd had a grand old time. When he was ready to go back to the studio, he asked if anyone was driving downtown. The campus was in Harlem, a hundred blocks north of Times Square. One of the reporters on the school newspaper had a motor scooter and lived in Greenwich Village. I mentioned it to Shepherd. "Great," he said, and hopped on the back of the scooter. He waved good-bye and had a broad smile. Years later, I was plugging a book and wound up at a radio station. Who was there, too, but Shepherd? I asked him if he remembered speaking at the school, and he said, "Sure do—got a ride home on a motor bike."

Barry Gray broadcast from a restaurant named Chandler's. That seemed to be standard for these late-night interview shows. Another late-night host was Bea Kalmus, who had guests at Hutton's restaurant. Another broadcaster, Bill Mazer, who was the most prominent name in sports-talk radio in the city at one time, did his show from the toney Oak Room at the Plaza Hotel. Gray had a formidable mix of A-list celebrities and politicians, and was a staunchly liberal advocate. I loved listening to his pro-labor exhortations, and the generally left-leaning Broadway types who were his guests, actors and writers and directors. But because of his liberal views he clashed with Walter Winchell, who tried to destroy him. Winchell called him "Borey Pink," and otherwise impugned his Americanism and his politics. Gray probably was the New York college kids' most popular personality in his day, but the pounding that he took from Winchell and others from the extreme right took its toll.

I remember listening to him one night, after Winchell finally had been discredited. Gray had a comedian on his show, and was poking fun at Winchell. Then the comic made a joke about how Winchell had treated Gray. Gray did not laugh. Instead, he spoke of how his life had been made a hell, and that doors had been closed to him, and that many people started to call him a Communist or fellow traveler. One night, several months later, I tuned in—and he was arguing with a liberal over liberal views. For Gray had turned into a conservative. I look back now, and it seems to me something like the Stockholm Syndrome affected him—to survive, he related to his captors. Subsequently, I was a guest on his show, plugging a book, I think. He was pleasant enough, but whenever we had a commercial break, he said something cynical to a member of his staff about their preparation, or about how the headset wasn't working properly. He was a pain in the ass.

Anyway, fast-forward about twenty years. It is the mid-1970s. I am a sportswriter for the *New York Times*. Television is king when it comes to airing sports events—except for hockey. That is still big-time on radio, unable, in the States, to make a television impact. I was the hockey writer for the paper. I had written five hockey books in five years. Perhaps twenty to thirty times a year, I would be the between-periods guest on radio or television broadcasts of the games—often I'd be on twice a game, once for the home team, and then for the visitors. Usually, these little spots were accompanied by gift certificates from the sponsors. There would be meals from restaurants, or sporting goods, or clothing, or simply twenty-five-dollar checks. I collected so many of these that I was able to barter some with another hockey writer who was in demand, Mark Mulvoy of *Sports Illustrated,* who went on to become the magazine's managing editor for many years. There was one gift, though, that I wish I hadn't taken.

I had gone on Rangers' radio broadcasts with my friend Marv Albert many times. He had not yet become a noted national personality, but in New York he was the play-by-play voice of the Knicks and the Rangers. He had a distinctive deep voice, was extremely knowledgeable about sports, which he painted extremely well, and produced imitated signature exclamations: "Kick save—and a beauty!" for the Rangers, and a resounding "Yes!" for a Knicks' basket. One of Marv's sponsors was none other than Chandler's, the Midtown restaurant that was the broadcast home of my old radio idol Barry Gray. As a present to me for going on the air as a between-periods guest, Marv gave me a gift certificate for two for dinner at Chandler's.

I was tremendously excited, not simply because this was a noted Manhattan restaurant but because it was an instance to get to visit a place I had fantasized about just a few years earlier. It was part of my big-city dreams, a place where celebrities sat, and smoke and drank and had sophisticated talk. My wife and I decided to make an evening of it. We did not realize what a night it would be. Our plan was dinner, followed by a new Woody Allen movie. We finished dinner, the check came, and I handed the waiter the gift certificate. He looked at it and asked me, "What's this?" The first pangs of doubt arrived with that question.

He brought over the maitre d'. He also looked at the piece of paper, then said, "Oh, we didn't do too well with this promotion, so we canceled it."

"Fine," I replied, "but before you did, you invited me to dinner."

He left to make a call, and came back and said, "We won't honor it."

In life, you don't get many chances to take a stand, even over issues such as a free dinner. I decided that this was my moment, and Chandler's, where I had spent so many nights over the airwaves, was my ground.

"Well, I won't pay for it," I said.

"I'll call the police," he said.

I told him to go ahead, figuring it was a bluff. He asked us to wait near the front door. Within minutes, two policemen showed up. The maitre d' told him I was "a wise guy," and trying to get something for nothing. I showed the cop the invitation.

"Just a minute," replied the officer. He called the station house. He got off the phone and told me I had to pay. I told him no. He said he would have to arrest me if someone signed a complaint.

From out of nowhere, the restaurant owner, who actually had signed my invitation in the first place, showed up to sign again—this time, putting his signature on the complaint. I was under arrest.

Well, the cops were very nice about it. "Should we cuff him?" asked the younger one. "Nah, he's OK," said the older one, as they put me in their patrol car. My wife, Roz, of course, could not come along for the ride. She was given instructions on how to get to the station house.

There, the desk sergeant was asked which cell I should go in. He looked at the complaint and said I could sit down near him while the paperwork was being processed. Just then, my wife walked in. Prisoners in holding cells, most of them prostitutes, could see her. She had a cold sore on her lips, which had turned into a welt.

"What's the matter, honey? Did he beat you?" one of the prostitutes asked, solicitously.

I got fingerprinted (the officer gave his gun to someone to hold; he explained to me that another cop had once been shot by the "perp" during fingerprinting). I was a potential cop-killer. Then the nice policeman said he was going to take my picture. I had to hold a board with a number under my face—you know, the mug shot. The problem was, the policeman didn't know how to use the Polaroid camera. My wife explained it to him, and he took the photo.

"You want another one for yourself?" he asked.

Well, after all this I was released after they asked whether I had a job, was I married, and did I visit my mother? These were all positives in their decision as to whether I should be released without bail. Two days later, my lawyer sued Chandler's for $750,000 for false arrest. I was at my desk at the *Times* when my phone rang. It was Marv Albert.

Marv has a forceful persona on radio and television. But I always thought of him as kind of shy. Once, at a New Year's party at my house, he seemed embarrassed when someone told a slightly off-color joke. At the time of the Chandler's incident, Marv was by no means a national celebrity—and thirty years from being a notorious one, at that. That happened when a spurned lover charged him with forcible sodomy. She also claimed he bit her on the back. He pleaded guilty to a misdemeanor-assault charge, did not serve any jail time, and his conviction eventually was wiped from his record.

But that was in the future. I picked up the phone to speak to Marv.

"Jerry, this is Marv Albert," he said. "Jerry—you've got to behave yourself!"

I tried to soothe Marv's fears that his reputation had been besmirched by one of his guests, me. I explained that I had legitimately tried to get the restaurant to honor the free dinner. We said good-bye, with Marv sounding a bit relieved. A few minutes later, my lawyer called. Chandler's wanted to settle for $7,500 and avoid a costly false-arrest suit. "Take it," my lawyer counseled. "All it cost you was some embarrassment."

I took it, and promised my wife a mink coat to compensate for her run-in with the ladies of the evening. Come to think of it, I still owe her the mink.

While Barry Gray was helping me imagine that one day I'd actually be able to afford to eat in Chandler's, a few notches up on the dial Joe Franklin was pioneering his "Memory Lane" broadcasts. He was the king of ham, but so sincere about the good old days. Every night he'd have a story about vaudeville, or a guest that was around in the 1920s or was a current star. He'd get them all, from Sophie Tucker to George Jessel, to Marilyn Monroe. And then one day I was part of that pantheon. I had just written a magazine article about the tennis star Chris Evert, and the publicist wangled a spot on Franklin's show for me to plug the piece. It was a hoot. I was on with a psychic and a street performer, the kind of guests he lined up as readily as he did Barbra Streisand. During one of the breaks, I said to Franklin, in jest, "You know, Joe, I've been on many shows, but you ask the most probing questions."

When we came back on the air after the commercial, Franklin said to me, "Jerry, you were just about to say something about other shows you've been on." So I repeated the compliment. Billy Crystal did a gorgeous Franklin imitation on the old "Saturday Night Live" shows, using Joe's patented phrases such as "Welcome to this fabulous panel." When I went on Joe's show again many years later, and mentioned the Billy Crystal take-off and how a younger generation now was becoming familiar with Joe, Franklin said, "I told Billy I was making him famous."

This time, Joe had me on by myself, introducing my "fabulous" book and discussing my "fabulous" career. Actually, the first time he had seen my book was at that moment, and he was reading the blurb on the back—a nice compliment from Coach Bill Parcells—and as he read it he spoke to me and the listeners at the same moment.

I was on his show following an interview he had with the octogenarian comedian Larry Storch (whose biggest role was on *F Troop*). Storch graciously stood up to say hello when we were introduced. He insisted he read me every day in the paper, although by then I was already retired and writing, just for fun, about once a week. But he insisted he knew my name and had been following my work for years. Was I going to argue with him?

Chapter 5

Life Imitating Art

Because my mother also was my companion when she came home, without a husband to share things with, and too tired to go out, she didn't talk down to me. She didn't have many friends, so she shared her thoughts with me. These were grown-up thoughts, on politics, on the entertainment front, on films, on radio.

When we listened to *Lux Radio Theatre*, which re-created well-known films, my mother would tell me tidbits about the stars—who was married to whom, who appeared in the original movie. The host, believe it or not, was the legendary director Cecil B. DeMille. Then again, for two thousand dollars a week, even legends would grab the money. The announcer introduced the show dramatically by saying, "Lux presents Hollywood!" and a parade of stars from the original films—Cary Grant, Judy Garland, Humphrey Bogart, among them—would reenact their roles in a one-hour broadcast. Supposedly, DeMille quit the show when he was asked to contribute a dollar a week to the union, to which he was philosophically opposed.

Thus, I got to know the great movies by listening to re-creations— even of silent movies such as *The Jazz Singer*. (It was billed as the first "talkie" but the only sound came infrequently, mostly during the musical numbers.) By the time I was ten, I had "seen" (on radio) such classics as *The Maltese Falcon* (Edward G. Robinson did Bogart's role), *Jane Eyre* (Orson Welles and Loretta Young), *The Philadelphia Story* (Robert Taylor in the Jimmy Stewart role), and Hitchcock's *Suspicion*. Even Judy Garland in *The Wizard of Oz*. I also lived only five blocks away from a dumpy movie theater that showed films long after their release date. Today, the Miller Theater probably would be called an art house, but back then, for twelve cents I'd see two movies, a cartoon, a newsreel, a serial, and coming attractions. To fill up the seven days, the Miller often showed classics from the 1930s and early 1940s on Mondays, Tuesdays, and Wednesdays—great old horror films such as *Frankenstein* or musicals such as *Forty-Second Street.*

And when I listened to campaign speeches of the irrepressible Norman Thomas, the perennial Socialist candidate for president, my mother told me she had seen him campaign in the thirties, and what it was like to be in an arena with thousands of people cheering a populist hero. The Marx Brothers, Bing Crosby, New Yorker humorist S. J. Perelman, Father Coughlin (the anti-Semitic radio cleric), the Algonquin Round Table with Dorothy Parker and George S. Kaufman—she knew about them all. And I did, too.

What else did I learn from radio? There were avenues for education that were unsurpassed, if suspect.

Take Friday nights, when my mother often went out, and I could go into her bedroom at ten o'clock and listen to Bill Stern. He was the most famous bull-shitter in all of sports. But he got my attention, and I anticipated his Friday night broadcasts. Little did I know his stories were made of imaginary happenings. He was famous, or infamous in the trade, I was to learn when I got into the newspaper business.

Stern was a nationally recognized play-by-play sports broadcaster. Often, he got the names wrong when he was calling the game, but on radio you could fake it. After all, no one listening knew that it was Jones who was running with the football and not Smith. Stern committed classic faux pas in his football broadcasts, and when he did, he figured out a simple way to right them. If he screamed into the microphone that Jones was running, but it turned out that it really was Smith who scored the touchdown, Stern would announce, simply, "Jones laterals the ball to Smith, who churns over for the touchdown."

Stern famously once attempted to soothe the hurt feelings of the pre-eminent horse-racing announcer, Clem McCarthy, who called the wrong horse as the winner of the 1947 Preakness. It was won by Faultless, but the colt's jockey wore red silks, as did the jockey of Jet Pilot. McCarthy yelled into the mike that Jet Pilot had won.

When McCarthy realized his error, he calmly told the listeners, "Ladies and gentlemen, I have made a horrible mistake. Babe Ruth struck out. Today, I did the same. I am in distinguished company."

McCarthy listened to Stern's solicitous words, and then replied in his signature gravel voice, "You can't lateral a horse, Bill."

But in my world, it was Stern's Friday night show that followed the live boxing at Madison Square Garden—the Friday night fights. Stern was sponsored by Colgate Shaving Cream, and a jingle would precede him, sung to the tune of "Mademoiselle from Marmontiers": "Bill Stern/ the Colgate Shave Cream man is on the air/ He's here again to bring you stories rare."

And then he told a tale with an O. Henry ending. I believed them all— you know, the one about the horse winning the big race with a dead jockey on his back, or the winner of the marathon who was blind. One that still haunts me was about an Alaskan trapper whose wife had died in childbirth during a winter storm. The child survived. But outside the shack, a storm raged for days and the hunter could not get any food. His baby was crying as the last of the stored milk was gone, and the pet dog was yelping with hunger.

So the hunter decided he had to brave the storm to find food. He strained to open the door against the screeching winds, and heard it slap behind him. He made his way into a white blizzard. Somehow, he was able to bag a squirrel or two. He found his way back to the cabin. When he threw open the door, he was greeted by a horrific scene: blood on the floor, on the crib, on the walls. The dog was looking at him from under the crib, blood on his mouth. The baby was gone.

Screaming "no!" the horrified hunter instantly understood what had happened. His faithful dog had killed and eaten the baby. The hunter aimed his rifle and shot the dog, killing him. At that instant, the hunter heard a moan. He looked behind the dog—and found the baby, alive. And next to the baby—a dead wolf. The dog had saved the baby's life by killing the wolf!

"And to this day," intoned Stern, "if you get to that part of Alaska, you will see a monument to that dog that saved the baby's life."

A great story, no? Passionate and sad, too.

Except that when I eventually went to high school, I read a famous Indian legend about the hunter who has to leave his wailing infant in search of food, and when he returns. . . . well, you know how it ends.

So Bill Stern had made up the whole thing.

We all remember those moments in life when we grew up just a little bit more. Hearing that Indian legend in high school was one of those moments of lost innocence for me.

Later, I was to learn he made up a heck of a lot of things. For I got to know his script writer when I became a reporter. The writer's name was Barney Nagler, an easygoing, underappreciated columnist who wrote for the *Morning Telegraph,* the horse-racing "Bible," and thus was known only to horse-players and journalists. Barney told me had written for Stern, "and I just made up a lot of stuff."

Did you know that Abner Doubleday, the "inventor" of baseball, had visited Lincoln at his deathbed? According to Stern, my hero, as Lincoln lay dying, he summoned Doubleday, one of his generals.

"Don't let them kill the great game, Abner," a dying Lincoln whispered.

And what about the guy who wrote "Sunny Side of the Street"? This one caught my attention because it wasn't about sports, although Stern did have a way of somehow inserting a sports event into his stories in order to justify the tale. After all, he was what we used to call a "sports-caster."

So according to Stern, a young fellow who liked writing songs was hit in the head at a baseball game, and suffered permanent blindness. But that didn't stop him from composing.

And that young man wrote an uplifting song about always staying happy and positive—it was called "Sunny Side of the Street." Even though he couldn't see the sunny side.

The only trouble with that story is that two legends in the music field—Jimmy McHugh and Dorothy Fields—wrote it, and neither was blind.

Stern loved to tell stories of youngsters who overcame the world's worst adversities. He ended their tales with, "And that boy grew up to be . . ." Thus, Thomas Edison, whom history records as being virtually deaf in one ear, received that handicap (according to Stern) after being hit in the head by a ball thrown by that famous fastball pitcher, Jesse James.

One night, Stern told an especially inspiring story that gripped me. It was about a boy who loved sports, loved to play more than anything. He had dreams of becoming a major-league baseball player. And one day he was playing ball with his little brother, who threw the ball into the street. The older boy ran after the ball, but he never saw the car coming.

The car hit him and badly injured his leg. He was taken to the hospital.

There, the boy heard the sad news: "Son, we're going to have to amputate your leg."

He would never play ball again.

But that boy kept up his interest in sports. Why, if he couldn't run or play, he'd write about sports or talk about it. Then, the punch-line, as I was beside myself wondering what had become of that poor boy:

"And that boy grew up to be . . . yours truly, Bill Stern."

God, I was so proud of that man.

There was a pause, and then his signature ending: "And that's the three-oh mark for tonight." "Thirty" was the last word written on typewritten stories back in the days of the linotype machine. In fact, I used to end my stories that way, as did we all in the newspaper business. It signified the end of the story, and clued the linotype operator into using a 30-point slug—that is, a spacer below it—to separate it from the next story. When Stern intoned "three-oh," it was past ten o'clock at night. I was ready for bed, but anticipating the morning and the weekend's radio adventures.

The Friday night fights that preceded Stern marked an hour of bonding between me and my Russian-born grandfather, Barney. For we both listened intently—me, because I knew something about the fighters, and was captivated by the excitement of the blow-by-blow call by Don Dunphy; my almost-deaf grandfather, because I think he heard the rising excitement in Dunphy's voice, and sensed something important was going on. Indeed, my grandfather would raise both feet off the floor in expectation of a knockout. When a blow landed, his feet crashed to the floor. It was a trait he continued when, finally, we got a television set with my bar-mitzvah money and he discovered a visual world he could relate to: wrestling. Yet, Grandpa listened to Dunphy on the radio as if making heads or tails of what was happening. I thought my grandfather had some sort of sixth sense—how could he know what was going on if he couldn't make out the words? Yet, there he was, rising out of his chair after a left hook crashed into a dazed fighter.

Dunphy's talent was that he spoke—really, dramatized—for three minutes, then had to spend the sixty seconds between rounds talking some more. It was quite a trick. Today's television announcers not only are freed from nonstop talk, they have a sidekick from the boxing business to do the analysis. But Dunphy was able to do it in the smoke and haze I imagined Madison Square Garden smelled and looked like. Because Dunphy didn't shout from the moment the bell rang, when he did raise his voice at moments of true excitement, he put a punctuation mark on the moment. You knew it was exciting for real, not simply a theatrical scream.

How could I have imagined that one day I would meet him, and that, eventually, I would write his obituary for the *New York Times*? I became the paper's boxing writer in the early 1990s, under the illusion that I'd travel all over the world covering Mike Tyson's fights. Promoter Don King had touted Tyson's release from prison as the beginning of a new era in boxing, with Tyson hammering opponents in locales from Argentina to South Africa to Thailand. I was the guy who was going to write about it in a most important paper. So I became the boxing writer, thinking I was going to do fights in a way that recalled those smoky Garden nights, where trainers named Sal or Abie handled fighters with nicknames like Irish Paddy or Tough Tony or Chico. For the world I planned to write about was the world I had only heard about as a child.

I don't know why I thought I could turn back the clock. Over the years, I had done quite a few boxing stories, most of them from Madison Square Garden. Once we left the 1960s, what was left of that old radio world soon died. Everything hinged on television, or theater-television, and then pay-per-view and, finally, cablevision.

And anyway, the old Garden I remembered over on Eighth Avenue had long been torn down and turned into an office building. But the first time I covered a fight there for the *Times,* on Eighth Avenue and Forty-Ninth Street, it was 1963 and only thirty-five hundred fans showed up. Indeed, the wrestling matches a few days earlier had attracted four times as many fans. Still, the place had a Broadwayesque feel, still inhabited by the Damon Runyon characters of *Guys and Dolls,* still teeming with pugs with flat noses and cauliflower ears. People milled in the huge lobby, a New York landmark as surely as the big clock in Grand Central Station. There were phone booths galore in that lobby, too—the arena itself had no places to make phone calls; I was told that was to prevent people from making bets on the fights or the basketball games.

I walked past the early arrivals, carrying my metal Olivetti portable typewriter, and headed for ringside. There, under the ring apron, was a wooden slat on which I could set the machine. There was one other person at ringside—my Western Union operator. He was an old guy who wore a green eyeshade. He sat down next to me and from a suitcase he took out a cigar box. He flipped open the box and took out a black telegraph key. Then he plugged something into a jack under the ring apron, and he was ready to start. He was going to transmit my story to the paper by Western Union telegraph—just as they had done a hundred years earlier!

He was a graduate of Western Union's railroad days, as were all the geezers who were using telegraph keys to transmit stories. When I typed my story, I handed it to him. He then proceeded to tap out, in Morse Code, the series of dots and dashes that would make sense to someone at the other end who was receiving my story. This was another Western Union old-timer sitting in the sports department at the *Times,* seven blocks south of Madison Square Garden. He also sat at a telegraph key, and when he heard the clicks coming in, he would type them on his ancient black Underwood. He handed the typewritten copy to the "copy desk," which then edited my story. From the desk, it went to a linotype operator who sat on a machine that had been at the paper since the 1890s. On this vestige from the Victorian Age, he typed about seven words a minute, each letter forming a letter made of "hot type." The finished words, sentences and paragraphs then were transferred by hand to someone called a "printer," who hovered over a form that was to be a newspaper page. By hand, he placed the type in the form, known as a "chase." He then tenderly pounded the type into place with a wooden mallet. Eventually, that chase made its way to another room which produced a copy of that page, and ultimately it was fitted onto our printing presses, which were two stories below ground, in New York City bedrock, so that the building didn't vibrate.

Ah, but the thrill I felt in pounding out my story while around me fans were howling and smoking, the smell of beer pervasive, the old man at the Western Union ticker clacking away. Cripes. Take that, Walter Winchell. I had joined the long line of truth-tellers, newspaper reporters. I was feeling a cosmic sense of oneness with my radio heroes, the guys in the World War II fighter airplanes shouting into their little microphones, or the newscasters with those true-American voices. Imagine—my story was being sent by Western Union. How much can a guy dream?

While I was busy pounding away, I would hear, from time to time, a woman's voice shouting advice—yes, constructive advice, not nasty—at the fighters. "Where's your left?" she wanted to know. "Use your jab!" she shouted. And then, every half-minute or so, she called out, "I want to see claret! Claret! Where's the claret?"

This woman intrigued me. I followed the shouting and discovered a petite gray-haired woman in a dress, hat, and gloves, sitting with her avuncular husband who wore a conservative suit.

"What's going on?" I asked. "What are you so excited about?"

"I want to see blood— 'claret,'" she explained. Well, I wrote about her, then saw her again at the next fight, and pretty soon she and her husband and my wife and I became friends. She was a great lady nicknamed "The Duchess" by her friends in the boxing business. She knew the athletic commission doctor, she knew trainers, managers, fighters. Her husband was a glove manufacturer; her father had been a leading magistrate in Puerto Rico. They lived on Central Park West, and boxing was their passion. She also had interesting ideas regarding liquor—"Scotch and milk," she'd command the bartender. "The Scotch is for fun; the milk's for my stomach."

The Duchess was only the first of a string of memorable characters I came across in the boxing business—indeed, they outnumbered the fighters. But what really surprised me when I took up residence at ringside was how dramatically different the in-person world of prizefighting was from the radio world it had inhabited in my youth. Yes, there was the rising excitement of the pre-fight introductions. And, yes, there was the noise and blood-pressure rise when boxers pounded each other. But even radio, even with the irrepressible Don Dunphy narrating, never could bring the flush to my face as the sweating fighters entered the ring. Or the pure fun of seeing the assorted pimps and prostitutes and Hollywood A-listers and wannabes who showed up in Las Vegas whenever Mike Tyson fought. At what other sporting event could I see Spike Lee in one row and Johnnie Cochrane in another? Or Nicole Simpson's sister sitting not far from Tracey Ullman? And the ladies of the evening in some sort of red plastic pants with see-through windows around their buttocks?

The first time I saw a fist smash into the other guy's nose, I reeled for a second, internalizing the hit. After a while, I became accustomed to the thuds and grunting, but never the gestalt of the scene. Then there was the moment blood flew out of the mouth of one of the fighters and landed on my computer, streaking it. I wiped it off with my finger, and then realized what I had done. In the age of AIDS, I had someone else's blood on my finger.

As I got deeper into the newspaper business, as I became the father of three (yes, I'll say it) fabulous children, the world of electronics was arcing forward. You could go through most of recorded history in ten-year increments and not find a heck of a lot that changed. But just a little more than ten years after I wrote my first Madison Square Garden story, the paper gave me another machine that was similar to my little Olivetti in one way only—it had a keyboard. Well, it also had the same blue color. But this was a computer, and the *Times* wanted me to be its first reporter to send a story by computer to the paper.

I can understand how performers on radio, perhaps newscasters especially, viewed television as the beginning of the end of civilization. The spoken word was going to be displaced by the visual, many feared. Certainly, a Winchell looked ludicrous wearing his jaunty fedora, while barking into a microphone on black-and-white television. And how do you get a televised Sky King to land on a secret airfield between mountain peaks, without having to pay for old film footage? And mostly, how do you imagine Superman or those other five o'clock heroes when you don't have to imagine them any longer?

As for me, and most of my colleagues, I looked at this computer as a corporate new-age gimmick. Something about it was sinister, and of course, the company had to have an ulterior motive in using this thing. Why, it didn't even take paper. You couldn't turn the roller to scroll up and down. You couldn't hit the return lever with your left palm to jump to the next line. It didn't make a rat-a-tat sound. And it weighed twenty pounds. Its screen was about the size of an index card. Its memory was a tape-recording disc, the exact same kind I'd use to record the kids' singing. When someone at the paper plunked down the machine at my desk, I asked my good friend and colleague Sam Goldaper, who had been writing since the 1940s, to try it. When the screen showed he had come to the end of a line, Sam whacked the side of the computer with his hand, as he would with a typewriter—thinking it would go to the next line. Of course, it did so automatically, without necessitating Sam to damage his hand.

Where would all this end? I enjoyed the tactile sense of rifling through stories, being able to edit them with a pencil—the thoughts transmitted from my brain to my fingers. Did poets type their thoughts? I wondered. It brought me back to the day my mother brought home that "three-way" Motorola radio.

So maybe I thought of this new computer as my old Motorola. Sure, the computer had some whiz-bang features, but it wasn't what I had grown up with. The office had some electronics whiz show me how it worked. This blue box was as wide as a pair of side-by-side laptops are today. It was about six inches high. It could do something, though, that my typewriter couldn't—I could delete a mistake, write over a letter, insert something, without moving paper or making it look messy. Words didn't exist in this computer. There were just a lot of letters and numbers in its own ether. I would have to get used to this new way of doing things, especially since I already had written six books and probably twenty-five hundred newspaper stories—all on a typewriter.

I had some dry runs on the computer, which I dubbed the Blue Monster, in the office. It had an external modem. You took a telephone and jammed it into rubber cups, one for the earpiece, one for the speaker. The way it was explained to me was that the light was converted to sound, which allowed it to travel over the phone lines. At least, I think that's what they told me. When the story was finished sending, a green light came on.

So I loaded the twenty-pound monster into my car and took it home. I fiddled around with it some more. It began to amaze me. I could leap in midstory to the top, or the bottom. I could find a word if I needed to make sure I wasn't repeating myself, without reading through the whole story. When I wanted to delete something, I didn't write over the letter with x's, as I did on a typewriter. I had a delete button. Imagine. I had to be careful about one thing, though. I had to jot down where on the tape the story was encoded. This was a cassette with a loop of brown tape, and the story could be on any place along it. But still, it could go fast-forward or reverse, just like a music tape cassette. Instead of going to another song, I was going to another story. Because I had the prototype model, it came with a few games, probably installed for the amusement of the programmers. "Hangman" was one of the games, although I was admonished that this was not a toy when the paper's computer guy saw me playing with it. But when my daughter Ellen, who was eight years old, saw it, she quickly figured out how to play it.

The next day I headed out to a prep school in deepest Long Island, where the New York Stars of the fledgling World Football League were training. It was to be the first site from where a computer-generated story would find its way to the *New York Times*. As I drove out, I inserted a Sinatra tape in the car's cassette player. Very fitting, I thought. At the training camp I interviewed the coach, the general manager, and some players, and was ready to write. I went to the car and toted the computer back to the team headquarters. I asked for a desk and a telephone and set up the machine and plugged it in. Problem. There was a spare desk to use in this nickel-and-dime operation—I had room to write my story—but the phone was in the general manager's office. And her desk was cluttered. I couldn't put the machine on it. What to do? I decided to rent a motel room and use the phone.

This was a cheapie motel. No desk in the room. I put the computer onto the bed, next to the phone on the night stand. I turned on the computer, dialed up my story, and was ready to go. I knew that back in New York, there were some important people waiting to see how this thing would work. One of them was A. M. Rosenthal, the executive editor. "Abe" Rosenthal already was a legendary newsman, a Pulitzer Prize–winning correspondent who now was transforming the *Times* in his executive's role. But I'm not so sure he was a fan of this newfangled stuff, which we at the paper called "automation." Indeed, "automation" was a buzzword in union negotiations, because the printers and the linotype operators and compositors and pressmen and proofreaders knew that their days were numbered, that this burgeoning age of electronics was going to sweep away their historic positions.

First, I telephoned New York to tell them I was ready. Rosenthal was part of a group waiting. There was also someone from the computer maker, and a good fellow from the paper named Chick, who was overseeing these first, tentative steps into electronics. I dialed the telephone, getting a momentary twinge when I realized I had to use a "9" to get an outside line. But that didn't affect what I had to do. I heard the blessed whine at the other end. I quickly rammed the phone into the coupler on top of the computer, and pressed a "send" button. I could hear the change in the sound of the tone, meaning it was going through. After about twenty seconds, I felt a change in the machine, and the green light went on. The story had been sent.

Elated, I called the office. "Are you ready to send it?" asked Chick. So they didn't get it. I thought of the classic Hollywood line, "Ready when you are, C. B." I told them I'd try it again. I dialed the office, placed the phone in the computer, got the green light after it was finished. Called the office—again, no story. I tried it a third time. When they told me they still hadn't received it, I heard Rosenthal laughing in the background. I suspected he didn't trust this new technology, but I certainly hoped he trusted me. Then, the fellow from the computer maker got on the phone. "Is there any interference out there? Is there a radio on, something like that?" No, there wasn't. But I heard a rattling noise coming from outside. I looked out the window—I was overlooking the parking lot—and saw that some workmen were breaking up part of the lot with a jackhammer. I relayed this information to the computer guy. "I think the vibrations are affecting the phone signal," he said. "Can you cover up the phone?" I looked around. The bed had a pillow on it, of course. "Let me try it again," I said. I dialed the paper once more, set the computer, put the phone in the cradle, took the pillow and placed it over the phone as if I were smothering it like the scene in *The Godfather,* and pressed the "send" button. After I got the green light, I called the office.

"Got it!" I heard someone shout amid relieved laughter.

The next day I picked up the paper, saw my name over the story, and felt immensely proud. It seemed odd to me that it looked like all the other stories on the page. That is, it had the same typeface, the same headline, the same spacing. Nothing leaped out from it proclaiming it computer-generated. It looked like any other story, ink on newsprint. And yet, this story didn't immediately alter the way *Times* reporters sent in their copy. It took another six years before the whole place was "automated" and everyone got computers. Indeed, even after a computer was placed in every reporter's hands, some reporters insisted on typing their stories on old-fashioned typewriters—and then retyped them on computers. They simply were happier and more at ease with something they knew. The words were more comfortable coming onto the typewritten page. I thought of those 1950s movies that refused to show someone watching television lest the film industry give the new medium legitimacy. Maybe if they didn't show a television set in someone's room, it would go away.

Well, the computer stayed and the typewriter didn't. And as the electronic world expanded, so did sports. They were becoming globalized—European basketball players made their way to the States, and eventually so did seven-footers from China. But my dreams of touring the world, as Mike Tyson's Boswell, never quite happened.

Tyson did get out of prison. But world capitals only a few decades removed from revolutions by peasants angry at money being tossed everywhere but at them weren't hungering to guarantee Don King fifteen million dollars to put on a fight. I wound up going to Las Vegas and

Atlantic City a lot. But along the way I met Dunphy, who was a truly ingratiating fellow. He was also getting along in years, though, and that meant the *Times* had something in mind for me.

Periodically, we check our list of "advance obits" to identify people who either have gotten seriously sick, or who have reached great age, and might not be around much longer. In checking these obits, an editor discovered we didn't have one for Dunphy. "We need his obit," I was told. This was an unusual assignment for me. It wasn't unusual doing an obituary—that was standard stuff. I had been schooled in writing them as a young reporter, when I learned to reconstruct a life from bare clippings. But this was someone I knew, and it was a ghoulish assignment. I soon ran into a small problem—no big deal if you're on most papers in America, but a very fine point at the hidebound and very self-conscious *New York Times.* Every obituary we write must include the person's date of birth, along with his or her middle name. Despite a few thick folders on clippings on Dunphy in what we called our "morgue," I could not find his date of birth. And it had become a point of pride with me to do the paper's bidding in these bits of arcana that helped make us such an imposing journalistic institution.

As luck would have it, I was going to the annual boxing writers' dinner that week in Manhattan. Maybe I could find someone there who knew Dunphy's date of birth, although I figured that was unlikely. After all, he had been born in 1908. At the dinner, I mingled with other people in the cocktail hour and I diplomatically asked my question. No luck. As I headed into the hotel ballroom for the start of dinner, someone came over and said, brightly, "Hi, Jerry!" It was, of course, Don Dunphy.

My moment. But how to take advantage of it—"Excuse me, Don, but I'm writing your advance obituary. You know you've looked a little pale lately. So I've got to know your date of birth for my story?" Hardly. Then I made up a little white lie, similar to some I've created over the years to get a subject to open up. This one was slightly different, though.

"Don," I said, "someone told me we share a birth date. I'm September 23d." Without hesitating Don replied, "No, I was born on July 5." I thought to myself, "Thank you very much, and sorry for asking." I wrote down the date on a paper napkin. I wrote his advance obituary the next day.

A few years later, when he passed away at the age of ninety, this is how his obituary began in the *New York Times:*

"Don Dunphy, the nasal-voiced announcer who brought the Friday night fights into America's living rooms in the era when voices had faces, died. . . ." Later on, it read, "He was born July 5, 1908." I had given Don a good send-off, as well as my appreciation for helping to make my own Friday nights so interesting when I was a boy.

In contrast to Dunphy's low-profile personality, many of the sports announcers not only spoke noisily but also were raucous in person. One of them was Harry Wismer, who was Ted Baxter before the character even was created for the "Mary Tyler Moore Show." He was loud, and a glad-hander, and had a heck of a voice and a colorful style. Something always was going on during a Harry Wismer game.

"Hiya, Senator Taft!" he'd shout into the microphone during a lull while doing a radio broadcast of Notre Dame football. Then he'd tell the listener that the famed U.S. senator had just poked his head into the box to wave at Harry. Chances are, Taft hadn't even been there. No matter, Wismer loved dramatics. He could cover up mistakes, too. Whether or not he actually had made the following call, the story has been passed down because, said people who knew him, it could have happened. Supposedly at an Army football game, its all-American hero, Doc Blanchard, was en route to a seventy-yard touchdown run. But from the moment Blanchard got the ball, Wismer screamed into the microphone, "Davis is running with it." Wismer confused Blanchard with teammate Glenn Davis, like Blanchard, a Heisman Trophy winner. Finally, when Blanchard got to the ten-yard line, the story goes, Wismer realized his mistake and shouted, "Davis laterals the ball to Blanchard, who streaks over for the touchdown."

Just a few months after I began my tenure with the *Times,* working as a copy boy, I picked up a ringing phone. "Hello," said the caller, "this is Harry Wismer. Who's this?" I told him my name. It was unknown to anyone outside of my family and friends and a few people in the office, who were impressed with the way I tore copy paper off the AP machine and got the coffee order right. I had yet to have a byline.

"Jerry," he shouted into the phone, "Congratulations—you're doing a great job!" A surreal moment for me, to say the least. The last time I had heard his voice probably was ten years earlier, barely into my teens. Imagine how you'd feel if someone you grew up listening to, or watching, tells you, the moment he meets you, "Congratulations," and then says how splendidly you've been working. "How did he know?" I wondered in my awe-struck naïveté. Wismer by then had left broadcasting, thanks to his marriage to a niece of Henry Ford's, and put his money into the New York franchise of the new American Football League. The team was called the Titans, and they were forever losing money playing in front of empty seats at the Polo Grounds. Wismer ran an ad hoc ticket office out of his Park Avenue apartment. People would be coming past the uniformed doorman to tell them they were visiting the Wismers'—and then plunk down money to buy seats for the football game. Eventually, he divorced and reportedly married the widow of American's most famous Jewish gangster, Abner (Longie) Zwillman. (How's that for symmetry: Wismer married to the niece of America's most noted anti-Semitic entrepreneur, and then hooked up with a Jew.) Wismer's Titans never made money, and he declared them bankrupt. Eventually they were bought by a group of wealthy racetrack people who changed the team's name to the Jets. Wismer died about five years later after fracturing his skull in a fall.

✳

Except for the fights, and listening to Dunphy on Fridays, virtually all sports that I heard on radio were daytime events. Baseball had yet to discover there was more money playing at night. Monday Night Football? That didn't come along until the 1970s. Once in a while, though, I turned the dial at 10:30 at night out of curiosity. For *Symphonette* was on WOR. Classical music was a noise to be avoided at my house. The one great piece of music I had ever heard played around my grandparents was on an old crank-up phonograph at their farm in upstate New York. It was of Caruso singing "Figaro." And it was more an object of derision than pleasure, a scratchy faint recording in a foreign language. No one understood it. No one cared for it. Indeed, they laughed at it, at the repeated "Figaro's," as if they were hearing a man who couldn't get the word out of his head.

Still, *Symphonette* intrigued me because the conductor was named Mishel Piastro, whose name conjured up a long-haired classical stereotype. I envisioned him in a tuxedo, somberly leading a phalanx of very serious musicians.

Some years later, I got a summer job with the *New York Mirror*, a Hearst tabloid that was the flagship of Walter Winchell. It was a raucous place, as a tabloid should have been, and was what I imagined the newspaper dodge was like. There were fedora-wearing reporters, drunk rewrite men—even the managing editor would send me to the local bar with instructions to "get my coffee—he'll know what you're talking about."

And there was a sob sister. She wrote about sleazy court cases and domestic spats. She was big and fat and she cursed a lot. Everyone loved her. Her name was Ara Piastro.

I once asked another copy boy where she had come from. "Oh, she's Mishel Piastro's daughter," I was told.

She was sort of fun, though. Just one of the guys. She joked a lot with the other reporters and editors. When you're a copy boy, as I was, you wait to be noticed, a sign that someone there understands that besides your ability to get the coffee order right, or to tear off copy neatly from the AP machine, you're also a journalist down deep.

My break came when Ara Piastro walked over to me and had a 150-page sheaf of papers in her two hands.

"Here," she said. "It's the New York City budget. Give me two paragraphs on it."

I spent the next five hours furiously leafing through the thing, double-checking the index to see if I could cull just seventy or eighty words about what was the heart, the meat, of this billion-dollar budget that covered education, the police, subways, streets—in short, two paragraphs of how to care for eight million people.

But I had learned my journalism lessons well, for I was able to produce a pithy, 120-word summary that I felt would perfectly fit in with the tabloid's mission: news, quickly and readably.

I walked over to her desk with the two-pound budget and my two-paragraph story (in triplicate). "Here it is," I announced.

She barely looked at it—and then said, "This goes in the circular file."

I had never heard that expression before. "What's that?" I asked.

"This," she said, and proceeded to dump the whole thing into the round trash can next to her feet.

Then she exploded in that manly laughter she affected—along with some of her colleagues. I had been had, like a freshman falling for a fraternity prank. My initiation into the world of journalism officially had started—by the daughter of Mishel Piastro!

How could I have guessed that this somber figure from Friday nights—at least, that is how I imagined him—would have had such a daughter? Or that I even would meet her?

As I tried to recall this story sitting down to write this book, I telephoned my old colleague at the *New York Times,* Larry Van Gelder, the noted culture reporter. He had worked at the *Mirror* once upon a time. I wanted an update on what had happened to Ara.

Larry told me she eventually married a mattress salesman, and had become the public relations director of the Girl Scouts. But when she was invited to a *Mirror* reunion almost forty years later, she was reluctant to show up. She had become somewhat of a recluse, and was in declining health.

Someone sent a car for her, though, and when she did arrive she was her old, ebullient self.

"When we drove her home, she got out of the car and she was almost dancing," recalled Van Gelder. "She died shortly after that."

The *Mirror* had another character whose history made an impact on me. His name was Jim Whittaker, and I got to know him because, when you're a copy boy, there's not much going on at noon. That was when he arrived, a gray-haired man in a double-breasted suit. He put down his coffee, took out his copy of the *Times,* and proceeded to do the crossword puzzle. This was very odd. Not many of the other reporters were in at noon. And he just sat there, by himself. Never said hello to anyone when he came in, nobody acknowledged him when he went home.

He had a quite distinguished air, and since I thought of myself as a journalistic project, not yet at a level I longed for, I was reluctant to speak to him. But one day I said something casually, and we got into a discussion about Chicago newspapering, where, it turns out, he had made his bones.

And then I discovered he was one of America's most interesting and celebrated newspaper people. Indeed, he had been married to a silent-screen and stage actress named Ina Claire, whose first name to this day crops up often as a three-letter crossword-puzzle answer in the *Times.* He also had been a newspaper music critic in Chicago and for the *Mirror.*

He is still quoted in the business for his review of a pianist, whose name has been forgotten, but not Whittaker's lead: "So-and-so played Beethoven last night. Beethoven lost."

Another classic first paragraph involved his wife, whose show he dared to review. This is how he started it:

"Last year when I married Ina Claire she gave her profession as an actress, but nothing in last night's performance would make me believe that was true."

As I got to know Whittaker, we spoke of the old Chicago days, and finally I got up the nerve to ask him how come I had never seen him writing—just the coffee, the puzzle, and his four or five hours at the newspaper.

He explained that he had done that every day for almost twenty years since 1938, when, he claimed, the *Mirror* punished him for his activity in the newspaper union with Heywood Broun, the leading figure behind the unionization of reporters in New York. Whittaker said they made him the paper's music critic, "which the *Mirror* needed like you need an extra set of thumbs."

"I'm not going to leave," he told me. "I like to sit here and remind them that I'm like an old bunion that can't be removed, but just lingers on to remind them how painful I once was."

And so I left the *Mirror* (to go to the *Times*) and retained that image of this old man sitting by himself at his desk, doing the crossword puzzle. A few years later, when I was a copy boy, I recounted this story to Gay Talese, who was a *Times* reporter. He suggested I try to sell it to *Esquire*.

So I went back to the *Mirror,* and spoke to the executive editor, whose name was Glenn Neville. I told him I was writing about Whittaker and wondered why he hadn't been given any assignments.

"So you're saying Jim hasn't been writing lately?" said Neville, who seemed surprised. "I didn't know that."

Whittaker wound up getting a bigger obit in the *Times* than Neville did, and I even contributed to it. I happened to notice on the day's agenda of stories that Whittaker had died, and I told the obit editor his "bunion" story. It made the paper.

The way Whittaker had been treated was not the journalism I had imagined when I listened to *Big Town,* whose hard-hitting but compassionate editor was Steve Wilson of "The Illustrated Press." For me, *Big Town* was, of course, a barely fictional version of New York City. The show had a wonderful cast that I was sure was the perfect mirror of the real newspaper: a society writer named Lorelei; the obligatory newsboy; a blind piano player; a driver named Harry the Hack. There was District Attorney Miller, who worked closely with Wilson and provided still another example of how a crusading newspaperman was a virtual part of city government. And since I read the *Mirror* as a child, I imagined the real-life editor probably was like Steve Wilson. The *Mirror* also was "illustrated," which meant it had pictures. But Neville was to shatter those comparisons and illusions.

It was another lesson learned in growing up, or at least growing into the real world, away from radio. I wonder if Neville appreciated Wilson's "kicker" at the end of the broadcast: "Freedom of the press is a flaming sword. Use it justly. Hold it high. Guard it well."

Radio teemed with newspaper stories, all of them feeding into my imagined image of what it must be like actually to work for one.

There was *Casey, Crime Photographer,* who was, according to the announcer's introduction, an "ace cameraman who covers the crime news for a newspaper in a great city." That city, of course, could be only one, I thought. The show invariably began where Casey, and I presumed other newspaper types, hung out: the Blue Note Café. Casey would arrive and start a conversation with the bartender, Ethelbert, who had a New York wise-guy's syntax and accent. The shows had titles such as "The Blonde's Lipstick," and "Murder in Black and White." Casey—Jack (Flashgun) Casey—often began his crime-solving when he came upon a murder scene to take pictures. He might see something strewn about, or, after developing the photos, see some suspicious object in the picture.

The character was played by another of those fabulous radio names—Staats Cotsworth, who, it turned out, also played another newspaper-type on another show, *Front Page Farrell.*

> We now present the exciting, unforgettable radio drama Front Page Farrell, the story of a crack newspaperman and his wife—the story of David and Sally Farrell.

Farrell worked for the New York Daily Eagle, and when I began listening, the show was essentially a domestic drama—husband and wife. Eventually, the couple turned into crime-fighters, which as any self-respecting journalist of the day (which I aspired to be) knew was his primary job. By the end of the show, he was working on the story—which he had helped solve—for Page One. But the show's signature dramatic moment came in 1945, when it was interrupted—to announce the death of Franklin Delano Roosevelt.

Because Farrell often spent his time eradicating crime by putting a spotlight on the bad guy, it was only fitting, I thought, that one of his sponsors turned out to be bug-killer. But not just any bug spray. This was called "The sensation of 1948." It was Black Flag, and contained ingredients including the new lab discoveries of D.D.T. and Chlordane.

It was, the commercial claimed, "The most effective spray ever developed for general home use . . . spiders, flies, moths, roaches . . . an invisible surface film for things that crawl." And, it turned out, things that fly or swim. For D.D.T. not only interrupted the breeding patterns of our national bird, the American Bald Eagle, it also had other unexpected consequences and, like Chlordane, eventually was banned.

The Big Story was a major weekly show, detailing how a newspaper got that "big story," with the reporters receiving a five-hundred-dollar prize from the Pall Mall cigarette company.

> The big story—here is America, its sound and fury, its joy and its sorrow—as faithfully reported by the men and women of the great American newspapers.

How could I not aspire to this fabulous profession after a start like that? The show dramatized a true story, although it kept only the reporter's real name. Most of the characters involved actually were fictionalized, as was the dialogue—thus, the made-up names of the characters. Perhaps the most famous segment was the one about a Chicago newspaperman who solved an old murder case. It was turned into the movie *Call Northside 777*. These heroic reporters used old-fashioned detective work after their instincts told them someone had been wrongly imprisoned, or the police had overlooked some important clues, or a politician was getting away with extortion. And of course, a cigarette sponsor was just about perfect. For the image of a newspaper reporter was someone wearing a snap-brim fedora, smoking a cigarette. It never was about the craft of writing—you didn't hear them discuss adjectives, as, say, Woodward and Bernstein did in *All The President's Men*. It was always about getting the story. Of course, that was what the Woodward-Bernstein book was all about, but they also showed some appreciation for the English language.

As for the cigarettes, well, this is how the sponsors of *The Big Story* made me feel as if smoking was not only fashionable and cool, but really quite good for you:

> Announcer One: Guard against throat-scratch.
> Announcer Two: Enjoy *smooth* smoking.
> Announcer One: Pall Mall's greater length of traditionally fine tobacco travels the smoke further . . .
> Announcer Two: Filters the smoke and makes it mild . . .
> Announcer One: Puff by puff you're always ahead when you smoke Pall Mall. At the first puff, Pall Mall smoke is filtered further than that of

any other leading cigarette. However, after 5 puffs, or 10, or 15 or 17, Pall Mall still gives you a longer filter of fine tobaccos—to guard against throat-scratch!

Announcer Two: Pall Mall's greater length travels the smoke further on its way to your throat—filters it naturally through Pall Mall's traditionally fine, mellow tobaccos—guards against throat-scratch.

Announcer One: Yes, Pall Mall's fine tobaccos give you a smoothness, mildness and satisfaction no other cigarette offers you. Guard against throat scratch!

No wonder that when I latched onto the *Mirror,* I already was smoking, although by then, the Marlboro Man had become my muse. My tenure at the *Mirror,* really just two summers while I was in college, was close to what I imagined this fabulous business to be. And I could smoke, along with the real reporters.

When I wasn't schmoozing with the exiled reporter Jim Whittaker, I sat at the communications center—a box with a bunch of telephone lines. The paper's "leg men"—the people in the field—would call in. "This is Flynn at the courthouse," someone would tell me, or "Ryan at the Shack." The shack was where the police reporters hung out at police headquarters. They all had Brooklyn accents, many of them had dropped out of public school sometime back in the thirties, and they all knew the politicians and police officials and, I assumed, the criminals.

I'd plug in a phone line and speak to them, then use a toggle switch to put them on hold or connect them to the editor they needed. Boy, these leg men had exciting jobs. The way the *Mirror* worked—and the *Daily News,* too, back then—was that these fellows in the field would phone in their information. They'd call in to one of the bank of rewrite people, who actually wrote the stories. Many of the pieces that appeared in the *Mirror* had two bylines—the leg man and the rewrite.

One of the rewrite guys was Jim, florid, quick-smiling, with a hunt-and-peck typing method that was the trademark of the paper's writers. After I was on the job for a few days, Jim called me over. "Would you go to the Greek's across the street and tell him you're getting Jim's coffee?" he asked me.

I went to the luncheonette and asked for Jim's coffee. I was given a plastic container, the kind they put coffee or soup in, that had been filled with booze. Then I presented it to Jim.

He set it down next to him. It must have contained six or seven ounces of liquor, but no problem. He'd sip from the cup as his face got redder, but his typing style never wavered.

The place itself seemed magical, as if torn from a radio script. It had started some thirty years earlier to chronicle the Roaring Twenties. And even though it was a poor second to the tabloid *Daily News* in circulation, clout, and style, it still hummed. These guys could find out anything and knew everybody. If someone was murdered in an apartment house, they could get the phone numbers of anyone who lived in the building, even if they didn't know the names. It was all about crime and sex. I once asked Neville how the paper justified calling a notorious gangster "a thug."

"He's a convicted thug," explained Neville, settling the matter.

The paper's newsroom was divided into little warrens of activity: the caption people—very important to a picture newspaper—were huddled together, as were those in the sports department. There was a bench and a desk for the copy boys, where we all sat and chatted, or made "books," which consisted of inserting carbon paper in between sheets of white paper for the rewrite men to type on.

One of the copy boys had a father who was a police reporter, and had some sort of contraption in his car that turned his radio into a loudspeaker. Once, as we drove around Greenwich Village in his Volkswagen, he used his special speaker to try to pick up girls on the street. He'd spot someone he liked and broadcast, "Hi, what's your name?" Everyone on the street turned toward the car, including the girl.

When I asked him if I could borrow the thing, he said, "Gotta be careful how you use it; it's for police business only." Still, this is how I figured Casey, Crime Photographer, and Front Page Farrell and all those other newspaper people on radio got around, and made out.

The *Times* was not so down-and-dirty as the *Mirror*, but it still had its bar. Gough's was diagonally across the street from the paper, on West Forty-Third Street. It was presided over by a drawn, florid man whose veins in his nose looked like a road map—Gough himself. The manager was his son. The waiter was John the Waiter.

This was the kind of place that Casey, Crime Photographer, inhabited. Cigarette smoke smacked your nostrils when you first opened the door. Then the noise. A few feet inside was the bar, where men with printer's hats (formed out of the newspaper) sat alongside reporters. Money was on the bar. It was the change the bartender laid down after you paid for a drink. You never picked up the change until you were ready to leave, for you were among honorable men. The bartender also cashed paychecks, and so every Wednesday at 7 p.m. the pressmen and the writers and the printers brought in their yellow checks to be cashed, always leaving something for the bartender. In the back there was a restaurant, with pork chops, scrambled eggs, macaroni and cheese, presided over by John, a horse-player.

So did Gough's make me a better writer; did it make others better pressmen or photographers? Did the smoke, the booze, the guffaws, the stories, help me in the business? Well, of course they did. Sure, a lot of the conversation was stupid and coarse. But I also became part of what had come before. I may have been a copy boy, but I was sitting next to and exchanging stories with Pulitzer Prize winners, or gray-haired, red-nosed printers who had been there since H. L. Mencken's heyday in the 1920s. I was in that stream that started when things were so much more fun. At least, that's what they told me. All I know is, when I was in Gough's, I was as comfortable and as happy as I had been sitting with my radio, hearing people make up stories.

Chapter 6

Weekends

When my mother went to work on Saturdays, I was left alone in the morning. But there was *Let's Pretend,* children's stories with a host of actors. It was sponsored by Cream of Wheat ("Cream of Wheat is so good to eat / That we have it every day / We sing this song, it will make us strong / And it makes us shout hooray!").

These were fairly sophisticated shows, as I remember. It had the classics such as "Sleeping Beauty" and "Hansel and Gretel."

Let's Pretend. How simple, and wonderful, the premise and its title. I knew I was about to be transported to another world, usually somewhere deep in a magical forest. What also was special about *Let's Pretend* was that you heard it in the morning, while you were alert—not as a bedtime story. So the words—the language—resonated as opposed to lulling you. And on radio, it always was about the words—not the looks, or the body language, or the editing cut from face to face to show a reaction. On *Let's Pretend,* the great children's stories—"Jack and the Beanstalk," "Aladdin and the Magic Lamp"—came into my house.

A digression: It's easy to show, and to see, anger or elation on television. Just watch if the lips are turned up or down. But to do this on radio—why, you had to listen to what they were saying, be aware of the inflection. And no television witch ever was as horrible-looking as the witch on "Hansel and Gretel" on the radio. For on television, the witch was a finite character—that is, it could be only just so horrible. She could never be more horrible than makeup or costuming made her.

But on radio, she could be green if I wanted her to be, have the nose of

Margaret Hamilton in *The Wizard of Oz,* or be ten feet tall, if I so chose. She was as horrible as I wanted her to be. Thus, in one show this young boy, and millions like me, had a lesson in vocabulary and imagination.

Around noontime, I'd call in my grandfather to listen to *The Answer Man.* The Answer Man was the world's smartest fellow. He would respond to listeners' questions involving arcana, or information about Timbuktu, or the world's biggest ship. Want to know the distance between the Earth and the Moon? He knew it. How deep is the ocean? The world's tallest mountain?

My almost-deaf grandpa, cupping a hand over his left ear (did that act as a sort of reverse megaphone, enhancing sound?) would chuckle in amazement as the Answer Man gave the height up to the last inch of Mount Everest.

"He is smart," my grandfather said.

"No, he must look up the answers," I said.

"He knows everything," said my grandfather, convinced that someone on radio wouldn't have the time to look up the facts so quickly. What did my grandfather know about tape-recordings—was the show live?—or researchers? The guy gave the answers on the radio, didn't he? He must have known what was going on.

Soon after, there was *Grand Central Station,* brought to you by Pillsbury's Sno Sheen Cake Flour. "As a bullet seeks its target," the show began,

> shining rails in every part of our great country are aimed at Grand Central Station, heart of the nation's greatest city. Drawn by the magnetic force of the fantastic metropolis, day and night great trains rush toward the Hudson River, sweep down its eastern bank for 140 miles, flash briefly by the long red row of tenement-houses south of 125th Street, dive with a roar into the two-and-a-half-mile tunnel which burrows beneath the glitter and swank of Park Avenue, and then [roar of a train and the whoosh of its airbrakes] . . . Grand Central Station! Crossroad of a million lives. Gigantic stage on which are played a thousand dramas daily.

This was a majestic opening, good enough to call me in from the streets to abandon my punchball game. "Crossroad of a million lives. Gigantic stage on which are played a thousand dramas daily." These last two sentences fed into our New Yorker belief systems—that because it happened here, it mattered more. Why, Superman lived here: his city was called "Metropolis," but we knew where it was. And Batman also was a resident, living in "Gotham." In fact, "Gotham" was a synonym for New York back in Washington Irving's time, and became the sobriquet of choice in the gossip columns, where the writers always were attempting to be clever. Anyone could write "New York," but "Gotham" gave the column an insider's take.

The shows about Grand Central Station really weren't about the terminal. That was merely the starting point—or arrival point, in most cases. From there, people went on their way, telling their tales. The stories had an O. Henry quality to them—a small-town girl comes to New York to become an actress, falls in love with the wrong kind of guy, and tries to extricate herself. They were small, well-turned stories, with actors such as Hume Cronyn and Mason Adams, and announcers such as the sonorous Alexander Scourby, who was to become the voice of *Victory at Sea.*

But the expression "crossroad of a million lives" still evokes significant memories for those of us who grew up in the train era, and especially growing up in New York during that time. And of course, my grandmother bought the sponsor's product: "All aboard for better baking . . . you're on the right track with Pillsbury."

The only other shows on radio I shared with my grandfather were the Friday night fights and Walter Winchell's frenetic Sunday evening broadcasts, accompanied by the sound of a Western Union ticker clicking away ("Good evening Mr. and Mrs. North and South America—and all the ships at Sea! Let's go to press!").

Boy, was that exciting.

The radio was the centerpiece of our living room. When Winchell was on, everyone stopped what they were doing to come in and listen. Even if we had guests over and were in the middle of dinner, we'd stop and go into the next room. There, we'd look at the radio, and give it our attention. You didn't talk when the radio was on—unlike watching television.

Somehow, it became important to us—not yet in Café Society, although I did have an uncle who was a bookmaker—when Winchell mentioned his favored friends, including his perennial host, Sherman Billingsley. Billingsley was a former Prohibition figure who owned the tony Stork Club. A parade of army generals and industry bigwigs made their names on Winchell's shows, and he peppered these with blind items, asking which movie star was stepping out on his honey, or which senator was halted for drunk driving. Winchell titillated as well as informed, and after listening to him, I'm sure my family thought it had grown much smarter, was now part of an insider's world. Once, he announced that he was going to give the name of a hot stock at the end of the show. Just as he started to name the company, the show ended, and I could hear him chuckling. I called the station—in those days the telephone operators at radio stations knew what was said on the shows, and indeed, callers' questions and complaints often formed the basis of programming—and was told it was a gag, that there was no hot tip.

The newspaper we got at home was Winchell's flagship, the *New York Mirror*. It cost two cents, and was published by Hearst. It actually was the other newspaper in the house. My grandparents read the Yiddish-language *Forward*.

In addition to Winchell, the *Mirror* was driven by its loud Page One headline, its back-page sports headlines, and the comics—as well as lurid crime-and-entertainment pieces starting on Page 4. Just as the Yankees and Dodgers fans had little common ground, and those of us who liked radio listened to rival adventure shows, New Yorkers of that era had their distinctive reading tastes—either the *News,* or the *Mirror.* Their comics did not overlap.

Some of the characters in the comic strips made it to radio or, eventually, television. And some leaped from radio onto the comics' pages. The *Mirror*'s comics included "Li'l Abner," a clever strip about country bumpkins. It also had "Joe Palooka," the world's heavyweight boxing champion. There was also "Steve Canyon," a pilot who had a blond streak in his hair. Even the horse racing page had a comic strip, called "Joe 'n Asbestos," a racetrack duo who often spoke in code when they wanted to give the readers a tip for that day's races.

Winchell was on Page 10 of the *Mirror* every day except Saturday. His radio style was like his newspaper column—punchy, with plays on words, anonymous quotes, right-wing rants, constant nods to J. Edgar Hoover and the FBI that was fighting godless Communism.

I was fascinated by the column for its wordplay, and the radio program for his sensationalist tone, even into my college years when, of course, I became quite liberal and against everything Winchell was preaching. By the time I started college, in 1954, Winchell was as noted for his ranting and raving as for any stories he broke. He had become a caricature with his hates and pet peeves. They included the late-night radio talk-show pioneer Barry Gray, whom Winchell labeled Borey Pink.

Then there was his feud with the expatriate entertainer, Josephine Baker, who claimed the Stork Club had discriminated against her one night. Winchell promptly gave her the moniker Josephony Baker.

I never ran across Winchell during my two summers as a *New York Mirror* copy boy. I did tote notes from the various editors to his secretary, Rose, whom many people suspected actually wrote some of his pieces.

Then one day in July, we had a big breaking story.

No, not the start of the landmark federal trial on integration in the South. The one about the actress Maureen O'Hara suing *Confidential* magazine. It had claimed she was necking in the balcony of Grauman's Chinese theater with her "Latin Lover."

I went to the Page One conference.

"Which is it—Maureen or integration on Page One?" growled Bobby Hertzberg, the make-up editor.

City editor Ed Markel thought for a bit.

"Integration," he said. "All caps. But put 'Maureen' under it, upper and lower-case, with a picture."

And this is how I came to cost the *Mirror* a fortune in circulation.

I went to the composing room with Hertzberg, a red-haired, wise-cracking newspaperman who must have seen too many movies about smart-ass newspapermen. The fellow making up Page One—known as a "printer"—took the "cut," the head shot of Maureen O'Hara, and tried to fit it into the hole designed for it. It was about an eighth of an inch too long.

"Take this cut to the photoengravers," Hertzberg told me, "and have 'em slice this much off it. But make sure you do it off the top of her head—don't cut the bosom."

Well, of course the guy I took the picture to put it in the wrong way. He sliced the boobs, not her hair.

When I brought it to Hertzberg, he contemplated the shorter bust of Maureen, turned the cut over in his fingers and growled, "Kid, you just cost us a hundred thousand readers."

Almost fifty years later, I was in a restaurant on the Upper East Side that fancies itself as a latter-day Irish pub, called Neary's. It is presided over by a sprightly gentleman, Jimmy Neary, who works on his fine brogue. We got to talking about the old days. He knew some of the people at the defunct *Mirror,* and I told him the Maureen O'Hara story.

"Did you know she called me New Year's Eve to wish me Happy New Year?" he said. "She's one of my dearest friends."

"Next time you see her," I said, "tell her the story."

"No, I don't think I'll do that," he replied.

Ironically, a few weeks later, my wife was in a bank in the neighborhood and heard two elderly women engaged in an animated conversation. One had a distinctive brogue. As my wife passed them, she looked at the one with the accent. It was Maureen O'Hara.

"You know," said my wife to the octogenarian, "you're still beautiful." Miss O'Hara smiled.

I had another *Mirror* moment a few years removed from my copy days there. I was working a game for the *Times* from the press box at Dodger Stadium in Los Angeles and a smallish older man, who dressed and looked like my grandfather, was sitting two seats away from me. He had a portable typewriter on the slab of wood that served as a desk. It was Winchell! He was in his seventies, a somewhat pathetic figure whose son had committed suicide and who had no great flagship newspaper. He was in effect writing for farm weeklies and small-town papers.

He had lost all his power, all his cachet. I'm sure he didn't chase fires in the chief's car the way he had in New York. Certainly, there was no midnight table at the Stork, where celebs would pay homage. I don't know what kind of story he was writing, but I suddenly felt sorry for this old guy pecking away on a portable. When I had listened to him over the radio, his was the most commanding voice I had ever heard. He was in control, a friend of the most powerful people in America, and he had the attention of my grandfather.

Now, in the press box, he was a lonely face, and I couldn't bear to see what he was writing. I never said hello.

He was one of the very few people I had heard on radio as a child that I actually got to see in person. Another was Red Barber. My earliest baseball radio memories are those of Barber, who broadcast my beloved Brooklyn Dodgers. He was immortalized in James Thurber's *New Yorker* short story "The Catbird Seat," in which his Southern, home-spun expressions such as "tearin' up the pea patch," and "sittin' in the catbird seat" form an important backdrop.

Barber was the voice of reason among baseball announcers, who were famed for their shrill delivery. But the Old Redhead, as he was known, never screeched, and when he raised his voice above a conversational tone, you knew something important was happening.

Now, fast-forward, and I am a young reporter doing my first Yankee game on the road, in Boston. Years earlier, Barber had switched to the Yankees' booth, a seismic event in New York baseball as reverberating as Leo Durocher's shift from managing the Dodgers to the Giants in the middle of the 1948 season, or Eisenhower deciding to run for president as a Republican instead of a Democrat.

I was still young enough to be a fan this day in 1964, and barely ten years removed from my teens. I guess there is something to the adage that you should never meet your heroes. Or, if you do, realize that this is the real world and not the fantasy you have created.

I saw Barber in the team's hotel, and introduced myself. Before our conversation could get under way, he started to tell me how he was being undercut by fellow broadcasters Joe Garagiola and Phil Rizzuto.

"How would you feel," said Red, "if your colleagues were talking on the air about a mistake you made?" He went on to complain about them, and I saw not this confident, kindly Southerner but a bitter man who had never struck this sort of note in my radio imagination. Here I was, feeling like a kid in front of a radio idol, and he's asking me for solace.

Now that I think about it, so did his longtime sidekick doing the Dodgers' games, Connie Desmond. He had a classic radio voice, with no regional accent, and a smooth if nondramatic delivery. I was a copy boy at the time, around 1960, and Desmond hadn't been doing baseball since the Dodgers had left for Los Angeles. I answered the phone in the office and the receptionist said a "Mr. Desmond" would like to see someone in sports.

I came to the reception area and was greeted by a quick-smiling Connie Desmond, who stood up, shakily. Clearly, he was drunk. That was my first disappointment after meeting him.

"Is Arthur Daley in?" he asked, in a classic alcoholic's slurring way. I told him that Daley, our Pulitzer Prize columnist, was off that day.

"OK, Jerry," said Desmond, putting an arm around me, "could you lend me five dollars?"

—✳—

Win Elliot hosted *Quick as a Flash*, that Sunday night show I used to attend with my mother. She got tickets to the broadcast from her brother-in-law, who was a salesman for the sponsor, Helbros watches.

Win also became the broadcaster for the Rangers' hockey team years later, when I got to know him. He was an engaging guy, father of ten children, I believe. Yet about a year after I began covering the Rangers, he was let go. He collared me one night in the Rangers' press room. Remember, this was one of those famous people I had grown up listening to not so many years before.

"Do you know why the Rangers fired me?" he asked. I had to admit I didn't. I wished he hadn't asked me. Well, at least Jack Bailey of *Queen for a Day* never called to find out why NBC didn't renew his contract.

I had other moments meeting with or talking to people who were iconic in their own way. I also learned I did not have to limit myself to sportswriting—that journalism is journalism.

I even became the *Times*'s TV sports columnist in the early 1990s, a job I found incredibly boring after writing my first few columns. It wasn't that I had disdain for televised sports. It was simply that I often sat at home by myself—no way was my wife going to watch sports—and armed with a yellow notepad and a remote control, I tried to make critical sense of events, or relay the history of the coverage, or put into perspective the difficulty of getting a shot from a certain camera angle.

This was nothing like the simple time of listening to my nightly fix of sports news. At 6:45 p.m. from Monday through Saturday over station WOR (710), Stan Lomax told you everything you wanted to know—including college baseball results if nothing else was going on.

"Hi, everybody, this is Stan Lomax with the day's doings in the world of sports."

"College hoops took the spotlight today," he might announce in a cheerful voice, and then launch into a detailed story of that night's games. If there was little going on, he not only would tell you about the St. John's–N.Y.U. baseball game but also he'd give you names of the battery—the pitchers and catchers. Although he was on for more than forty years, all those hundreds of days a year, he did only one live interview a year—with the director of the Millrose Games, the annual track-and-field event at Madison Square Garden.

But while Lomax was the most noted sports news show, we didn't really have many opinions of sports on radio. Then, in the mid-1950s, the Brooklyn Dodgers' flagship station, WHN (1050), began a broadcast called *Warm-Up Time*. It was a round-table discussion of the game coming up, but quickly became a lightning rod for all sorts of sports talk. This may have been the first—certainly, it was the most important because of its market—of sports-talk radio as we know it today. I'm not talking about an individual broadcaster. I'm speaking about having a mix of people getting together to argue. At that point, there were no phone-in callers. At least, none got on the air, although I know they used to call the studio when they had something to complain about. I used to listen avidly, for several of the panelists were Dodger fans. But one in particular was, somehow, a Giants' fan.

He was Marty Glickman, who became a friend when I started to cover the Jets' football team and he was their play-by-play announcer. Marty, though, was a well-known New Yorker, the voice of the Knicks' basketball team, a former high school and Syracuse University track star who inadvertently became a part of a much larger historic saga.

For he was one of the two Jewish runners on the 1936 U.S. Olympic team who were unceremoniously bounced just before the games were to begin in Hitler's Berlin. It has always been speculated—and in recent years, many have offered proof—that the reason Marty didn't run was because the head of the U.S. Olympic delegation, Avery Brundage, did not want to antagonize Hitler. So Marty's spot on the 4x100 relay team was taken by a fellow named Jesse Owens.

Sixty years later, when Marty was voted into the Jewish Sports Hall of Fame, I interviewed him for the *Times*. It was the first time I had ever heard him refer to 1936 with some bitterness. But a moment later, he was his cheerful self again. He enjoyed calling me "Keed."

From time to time, one of the panelists on his old radio show was the tennis star Gussie Moran. She had became iconic, though, by wearing lace panties at Forest Hills, and forever after was known as "Gorgeous Gussie Moran."

Even with her less than strident tone, the show became a paradigm of the New York fan, noisy, bickering, in-your-face finger-pointing and jabbering. And why not? This is what we did all the time, especially in discussing baseball. None of my friends actually went to the games—after all, a seat in the bleachers cost sixty cents at Ebbets Field—but we could argue after listening to the game on radio. The group, Glickman, Moran, a fellow named Ward Wilson, and another named Bert Lee, Sr. (followed, eventually, by Bert Lee, Jr.), also had a post-game show called *Sports Extra*. This was filled with second-guessing of managerial decisions, but mostly it was about arguing with one another and seeing who could shout the loudest.

What broadcasters said, mattered. Why, when Dizzy Dean was tapped to be a Yankees' broadcaster, it was as much for his folksy chatter, his nasal rendering in song of "The Wabash Cannonball," and his unique syntax and grammar as for his Hall of Fame pitching credentials.

Everything went well with Diz and the Yankees and their fans until one game he described a player as having "slud" into second. That may be a fine past tense for "slid" back in Diz's hometown of Lucas, Arkansas, but it was not acceptable in the New York City school system. And so teachers and other educators raised a cry with the Yankees—who always thought they were the classiest sports team, anyway—and poor Diz soon was gone from the broadcasters' booth in the Big Apple.

These were the kinds of impact stories we talked about daily. So every evening after supper in the summertime, after having digested that day's game—night baseball still was a novelty—we met at the candy store and sat on the newspaper stand. We were waiting for the evening delivery of the "morning" papers—the *News* and the *Mirror*.

Each paper was two cents, and each came by truck about half an hour apart. Until they arrived, we had formed an al fresco panel discussion, with none of the niceties of language that marked the *Warm-Up Time* radio show. New York, after all, was the baseball capital of the world. Hard to believe, but every year from 1949 to 1958, a New York team was in the World Series. This was the era of Willie, Mickey, and The Duke. Thus, we waited for the papers to punctuate the day's radio broadcasts, to put into perspective what we had heard. We weren't disappointed, for the tabloids led their back page with baseball every day, seven days a week, from April through October. My own patois of sports was formed by the tabloid writing, which I thought was the way sportswriters were supposed to sound. Baseball broadcasters on radio could be dramatic and talky, but their adjectives were quite scholarly. Oh, they'd talk about a batter trying to get a pitch in his "wheelhouse" or the "southpaw slants" of a pitcher, or of saying "laying the lumber."

Ah, but once the tabs arrived, a new world of language unfurled. It started on the back page, with the singular shorthand these papers used, and which, I'm sure, would have driven crazy an immigrant who was trying to learn English.

"Bombers Topple Pale Hose," a headline might shout about the Yankees having defeated the White Sox.

Or "Flock Defeats Birds," the *Mirror* headlined—meaning only one thing: the Flock (the Dodgers) had defeated the St. Louis Cardinals. Then again, the "Jints Squeeze by Bees" was a shorthand way of saying the Giants narrowly defeated the Boston Braves (perhaps even using a squeeze play).

And when I flipped the pages backward, to read the stories—why, that was English! Or at least sportswriting. Every cliché from the first recorded instance of a man swinging a stick at an offering from a pitcher sixty feet, six inches away made it to the tabloids. Balls that were hit between left and center were "tweeners," and a player wouldn't simply steal second base, he'd pilfer it, and a fastball pitcher was throwing heat, while someone with a less powerful arm was hurling up junk, and a batter used a wagon tongue to swat the horsehide, which could result in a dribbler, or a high can of corn, not to mention a circuit clout.

Teams wouldn't simply win—they'd throttle, triumph, nose out, deck, jostle, eke out, trample. "Lose?" No way. You'd blow it, drop, flail, fall, sink, stumble. Why, when I finally got a chance to actually meet my first major-league player, Duke Snider, I summoned all my sporty syntax. I was a senior in high school in 1954, and had been invited along with the sports editors of other school newspapers to meet the Dodgers' star before a game at Ebbets Field.

It was nice and cozy, behind home plate, about thirty of us and the Duke. The p.r. guy asked for questions, and I, of course, had mine, honed after years of reading the *Mirror:*

"Duke," I asked, "what's the longest smash you ever clouted?"

That, I thought, was how sportswriters should ask questions.

The Dodgers consumed not only me, but the people in my neighborhood, of all walks. Listening to the Dodgers on radio was a daily event. There was an older man across the street—"old" to me back then; who knows? maybe he was fifty, maybe sixty—known as Mr. Tin. I think it was short for Mr. Tinefsky. Well, every Dodger game found him sitting in a green beach chair on the Brooklyn street, outside his four-story, walk-up apartment house. He kept a little brown Motorola portable radio on his lap, and he wore a green eye shade. He'd turn on the Dodger game while holding court on the Brooklyn sidewalk. He spoke with a Yiddish accent, but the Dodgers had become his team in his road to Americanization—thanks, I'm sure, to radio. It chronicled their daily doings, their highs and lows, for two to three hours a day. It was perfect for this man who didn't work. I had heard he had survived the Holocaust and had some mysterious disorder that kept him from working. But he certainly was animated listening to his "Brooklyns" day in and day out, in his little corner of the Brooklyn world, oblivious to the buses that roared past him in the streets just a few feet away.

And then, one day in 1951, an event turned Brooklyn upside down. It was a game that will live in infamy, heard, I'm sure, by everyone in New York who cared about their team.

My Dodgers had built up an insurmountable lead by mid-August. At one point it reached thirteen and a half games. The Giants? It was impossible for them to overtake the Dodgers, wasn't it? Yet the Giants went on a spectacular winning streak, and the Brooks started playing only .500 ball. The Giants inched closer, and then they tied the Dodgers, forcing a three-game playoff. It went to Game 3, which was played, of course, in the afternoon.

My French class at Thomas Jefferson High School ended at 3:50 p.m. Everyone dashed into the hallway and someone hauled out a portable radio. The Dodgers were leading in the bottom of the ninth by two runs, there were two out, two runners on, and Ralph Branca had just been called in from the bullpen to face Bobby Thomson.

There was a roar as Thomson connected, and then the hysterical Russ Hodges, the Giants' broadcaster, kept screaming into the microphone, in what became a famous litany, "The Giants win the pennant, the Giants win the pennant, the Giants . . ."

The time was about 3:54 p.m., memory tells me. I walked home crestfallen not only for the loss of that moment but also for the heavy burden of being a Dodger fan at this moment in time, of having been disappointed by the only sports heroes I ever had.

It was ten blocks from my high school to my house. As I got near my corner, I saw Mr. Tin sitting there, and I imagined how crestfallen he must have been. Instead, he was wearing a Yankees' cap. The son of a bitch had switched allegiances because of one swing—and the body hadn't even been cold for fifteen minutes. Mr. Tin never spoke of the Dodgers again, and I never again saw him outside with his radio when the Dodgers were playing.

Hodges's infamous (to me) call was heard only on WMCA radio, and back in 1951 radio broadcasts were not routinely taped. But a Dodger fan, ironically, did tape it. He eventually sold it to the Giants' sponsor, Chesterfield cigarettes (the "h" or the "e" would light up in "Chesterfield" on the center-field scoreboard to indicate if a batted ball were ruled a hit or an error). Chesterfield produced a disk of Hodges's call that it sent to candy stores all over America. That is where I heard the replay of the most emotional sports moment of my life. In the candy store across the street from where I lived, where the owner, Teddy Pilo, played the record and started to laugh.

"Where's Mr. Tin?" he asked. Pilo hated a turncoat.

I had lost a three-dollar bet on the Dodgers, having put up my money during August when they had that huge lead. Forty years later, I wrote a story about the anniversary of Thomson's shot against Branca. In a way, it was closure for me. I felt an intimate part of their shared moment. I called Branca. I called Thomson. They were about to go on the Home Shopping Network to sell signed baseballs. I chuckled as I sat down to write remembrances of that home run past and the effect it had on people's lives. Here I was, getting paid for it. I finally had made back that three dollars.

✴

By the time I got to the *Times,* I had toned down my breathless sports prose, in speech and on paper. I found many outlets for writing in the paper, which encouraged cross-sectional stories—that is, it wasn't unusual for a writer from one section to do a freelance piece for the Sunday Real Estate section. I was always on the lookout for these chances, which also brought more money in addition to a different kind of exposure.

So, ensconced as a sportswriter for some years, one day when I was reading about a reunion of the *Father Knows Best* television characters, I thought it would be a fine idea for a story, which I proposed for the Sunday Arts and Leisure section. They accepted it. I got in touch with all the people on the show, Jane Wyatt, who played Mrs. Anderson, and the actors—all grown up—who played the children, and, of course, Robert Young.

I had a fascinating conversation with Young, especially when I asked him about his portrayal of "Mr. Anderson—'father.'" He told me he had been an alcoholic, and "hardly a nice person," in his words. But the role of the all-wise parent got to him personally.

"I wanted to become the person I portrayed on television," he admitted. "And I did." After I wrote the piece, I got a nice note from Ms. Wyatt. Years later, I read about Young's failed suicide attempt—he attached a hose to his car's tailpipe in his garage—and in 1998 he died of respiratory failure. I hoped he had become the person he wanted to be by then.

I also touched the world of make-believe when I was writing a base-ball book sometime in the 1980s. I needed to interview Jimmy Piersall, a player famous in his time, and nationally noted for an autobiography about his mental illness called *Fear Strikes Out*. It was made into a movie starring Anthony Perkins (who threw left-handed, awkwardly, with a "girl's motion." But the film editors reversed the print since Piersall threw right-handed).

Piersall was a willing interviewee, and we had a grand time. I noted that Perkins hardly was the athletic sort, and Piersall readily agreed. He also said that Tab Hunter had portrayed him in a made-for-TV version of the book.

Said Piersall: "Here I am, a married guy with nine children—and two fags play my life in the two movies about me."

Chapter 7

News

Of course, kids of ten or eleven or twelve wouldn't be caught dead today watching the news on television. Why, my brilliant grandchildren scream "no!" when I suggest turning off *Jimmy Neutron* for CNN. There is no regular time for children today to watch the news. It is not part of their experience, or interest.

But it was mine, and my friends'.

Perhaps today's youngsters don't care about the news because they don't have to listen to it. By that I mean there are alternatives. There is always a children's program on somewhere at, say, 5 p.m. or 6 p.m. or 6:30, when the local and network newscasts start. There are dozens, if not hundreds, of channels to choose from at any given moment.

But on radio back then, the dial was finite. And the news was everywhere at the same time, say, at 7 at night. No kids' stations to turn to. In fact, there were never any children's stations, merely children's programming for a specific time every day.

There was another reason we listened to the news in the forties—we were at war. Even when I was eight or nine years old, I recall listening to the reports of the war, where the fighting was, with the names of the strange places—battlefields—where "our boys" were.

War was all around us—even in the haven of Brooklyn. I had a friend who claimed he could tell by the sound of an airplane whether it was one of "ours"—luckily, one of "theirs" never flew over Brooklyn, as far as I knew.

And in our weekly savings books that each child in New York City brought to school, banks would slip into the deposit envelope a baseball-trading-card-size picture of an American or Japanese or German fighter plane. We would bring our bank books in on Tuesdays, and get them back on Fridays. We also got photos of the airplanes when we bought twenty-five-cent "victory" stamps, which went to purchase a "war bond." If you bought $18.75 worth of stamps, you'd trade them in for a $25 bond. Children all over New York, and, I suppose, America, were thus helping the war effort by lending money to the government in this way. It shouldn't be surprising, then, that I'd be listening to the news—I had a stake in the outcome.

Some of the broadcasters were breathless—such as Drew Pearson, famed for his predictions. They weren't necessarily accurate, but they were fascinating. One show from 1944 (brought to you by the laxative Serutan, "natures spelled backwards") included the following:

"Hitler may set the English Channel on fire to prevent invasion. . . . President Roosevelt is not insane, nor is he near death. . . ."

While I listened to the virtual blow-by-blow unfolding of the war, I was also aware of a daily dose of advice: "never waste soap," for example. The ingredients were needed for the war effort, as Duz explained:

> Work for victory at your dishpan by saving soap. Soap contains raw materials. Never waste them. In war-time, never waste anything.

Thus, my mother learned about making a soap mitt—taking a washcloth, and filling it with slivers of soap, kneading them together. Instead of being at the end of their life, the soap slivers virtually were reborn. We did this as diligently as some people took care of their "victory gardens," home-grown vegetables in places like window boxes or front lawns, so that farmers wouldn't be as strained in producing food for the millions of people in the military.

And while we didn't have a car, I knew we should conserve gas. We also crushed empty food cans with our feet, put them in boxes, and gave them to the trash collectors, who I assumed then brought them to ammunition factories to make bullets.

I knew the names of Pearson, or Winchell, or Edward R. Murrow. Would today's ten-year-olds know Rather? Or Chris Matthews? Or even Larry King? But my guys were simply part of the radio family I was growing up with. There was even an odd show titled *Wendy Warren and the News,* which came on at noon. It was a soap opera but had an unusual aspect: the first three minutes of the program was an actual news broadcast (by Douglas Edwards). Then, somehow, it made a segue into the fictional show of "Wendy Warren's" adventures as a broadcaster.

At the end of the war in 1945, Murrow broadcast from the concentration camp at Buchenwald, bringing to me, a nine-year-old, the first awareness of what had been going on. Murrow warned us, "If you are at lunch, this will not be pleasant." He described walking through one barracks, where frail inmates could not get out of bed, but when they saw him, started to applaud—"It sounded like the hand-clapping of babies," he said. He also spoke of prisoners too weak to walk, so they crawled toward the latrines. "I saw it, but will not describe it."

This was the harshest reality yet that radio had brought me, a new way of looking at the world that even as a child who had grown up hearing about battles and victories and loss, was something quite new. This was not a silver-screen depiction of horror or gallantry. I did not then know the phrase "man's inhumanity to man," but for the first time I had a sense that this was possible.

In August that year, with the Japanese about to surrender, I had the sense that all this was happening because we were ultimately the good guys. If you listened to the news on radio, you'd hear the announcer talk of some important event happening on "Eastern War Time."

Murrow headed a team of savvy CBS journalists (known, I was to find out, as "Murrow's Boys"). They were in critical parts of Europe. At times, he had them all on in a sort of conference call, and when he wanted them to speak, he'd call on them by their second names—"Sevareid, what's the mood of London?" His other "boys" included William L. Shirer, Charles Collingwood, Larry LeSueur, Richard C. Hottelet, Robert Trout, and Howard K. Smith. After the war came Daniel Schorr, still broadcasting almost sixty years later on National Public Radio. Besides their wonderful names—I never again believed news broadcasters could be anything less than grand—they had the voice of authority.

Every night I would hear one or more of these broadcasters, often with the sound of war in the background, and they gave me a sense that what these journalists did mattered. Their mission was all the greater because of the feeling of personal danger that all of them were undergoing to bring me the news. To a degree, they were heroic in the same manner as my fictional 5 p.m. guys, the Jack Armstrongs and Captain Midnights. Their broadcasts helped shape my ideas of what was important in the world, and what I wanted to do. Imagining what it was like with shells bursting nearby, I thought their lives as dramatic as Sky King's—but perhaps for the first time, was able to understand that there was after all a difference between kids' shows and real life.

Gabriel Heatter's legacy is not so great as Murrow's, but for those of us who remember waiting to hear what the "good news" was in the midst of worldwide chaos, he was an important figure.

I found out only later that he actually lived in my Brooklyn neighborhood at one time. But his voice had none of those Brooklyn-bred "dese" and "dem's"; instead it had that suggestion of the upper crust, with a broad "a," and that, of course, put him in a quite different neighborhood in my mind. When he broadcast the German surrender, he declared, "Now the guns are quiet everywhere in Europe, and the lights are on." Then he added, "Here's my forecast: We will beat the Japs before President Truman is sixty-two years of age. He is sixty-one today."

When you hear the word "Japs" today you cringe. But it was no more than a casual way of regarding a hated enemy—just as the Germans were "the Krauts" or "the Hun." Calling them "Japs" did not, I think, connote a hatred or distrust for Japanese Americans. Heatter, and all of us, were talking about the enemy forces in Japan. Today's announcers and journalists speak or write of "militant Islam" without actually using the word "Arab," or of saying something derogatory about Muslims (although members of Congress repeatedly referred to "camel jockeys" and "the Ayatollah Cockamamie" during the first Gulf War).

Before the phrase "politically correct" had been invented—or even became an eponymous television show—there was a sensibility and politeness displayed by warring ideologues, even to the pundits who opposed Franklin Roosevelt. One of those was Fulton Lewis, Jr., who would be described today as an arch-conservative, and who was on the radio for fifteen minutes every night. He was a fan of Father Coughlin's, and supported Charles Lindbergh's pre-war isolationist beliefs, even admiring some of Hitler's ideas. Lewis opposed most of Roosevelt's New Deal policies, many of which tried to put the common man back on his feet.

But when Roosevelt died, Lewis's broadcast began, "This nation has suffered this day a staggering loss. . . . President Franklin Delano Roosevelt lies with the problems of this nation finally lifted from his shoulders."

It is hard to imagine the anti-Clinton gang saying something similar if he had died in office, or George W. Bush–bashers mouthing such regrets had that happened.

My daily dose of news included listening to the grandly named Hans von Kaltenborn (known as H. V. Kaltenborn), who had a clipped style of delivery but whose background was fascinating—he had run away from home to fight in the Spanish-American War; he had been a tutor to one of the Astor children; he had broadcast from Europe before the beginning of World War II. In some circles, Kaltenborn was considered a pioneer in radio editorializing—he offered opinions along with the news.

Kaltenborn was such a powerful national figure that Harry Truman, before his inauguration, even read an excerpt of Kaltenborn's election-night broadcast, making fun of his delivery as Kaltenborn proclaimed several times that Truman would never be able to capture the electoral vote.

Chapter 8

Why They Mattered

I see that what my weekday-evening fictional heroes had in common was an upstanding-ness. Also, the shows told a good story. And if there were family verities as well, so much the better for me. But what was there about these characters that made them such an important part of me, of my school day? Let me see:

The Lone Ranger put on a mask after he was ambushed by the Butch Cavendish gang and rescued by an Indian, and rode away at the end of each thirty-minute adventure while a befuddled but grateful lucky soul asked, "Who was that masked man?" Music up: "The William Tell Overture."

What did I know of Rossini, who wrote it? As far as I was concerned, "The William Tell Overture" was called "The Lone Ranger Music." Indeed, I was quite surprised to learn it was considered "classical music" when I entered the fifth grade.

For at Public School 158 in Brooklyn, and at grade schools all over New York City, millions of us children were introduced to music classics with excerpts from the canon of the most popular themes. We were required to memorize them by the time we were in sixth grade—if not, we were told, we would not graduate.

That's right, passing the Music Appreciation test, as it was known, was critical to graduating. If we didn't know the Toreador song from *Carmen*; Tchaikovsky's first piano concerto, "Waltz of the Flowers"; "Danse Macabre"; "Amaryllis"; "In A Country Garden"; "March Slav"; "Humoresque," and "Anitra's Dance"—why, we'd be left back.

This exposure to music—and that's really all it was, hardly an appreciation of it—was part of our acculturation. After all, we were the children of immigrants. What did I know of music by the three B's? "March Slav"? Or "Amaryllis"? The first time I heard "Amaryllis," and learned it was written by Ghys, I thought the composer spelled his name "Geese."

Similarly for Saint-Saëns. When I saw the name written, I assumed it was pronounced "Say-ens." And Tchaikovsky? Never mind.

His Piano Concerto in B-Flat Minor had been popularized as "Tonight We Love," with words added. Indeed, it was the theme song of a noted band leader of the day, Freddy Martin. That's how I knew it. One morning in the school auditorium—packed, as I recall, with about three hundred kids—we were given some more music appreciation.

The teacher put a black disk on the phonograph, and out came the familiar strains of what I knew as "Tonight We Love."

"Who knows what that is?" the teacher asked.

My hand was the first in the auditorium to be raised—actually, I remember thrusting it confidently so that it couldn't be missed. She called on me, and I responded, "Tonight We Love."

"No—anyone else have another idea?" she said.

When some smart-ass sixth-grader got it right with the Tchaikovsky, I was incredulous—even worse, I had a moment so embarrassing it might as well have been in one of those perpetual dreams about walking into school in your pajamas, or naked. So I learned my Tchaikovsky the hard way. But the Americanization of all us poor or culturally deprived kids didn't stop at music. And radio often was the common denominator, our window on this great country that seemed foreign to us, tied to our neighborhoods.

So the New York City education system was geared to taking us out of our self-imposed ghetto, cleansing us of our ignorance, teaching us the rudimentary requirements of civilization as practiced on these shores and not in some European village where your mother and father had got their shoes covered with horse manure in the muddy, unpaved streets and had to wait until Saturday night to get a bath. Indeed, self-help Jewish organizations were everywhere to show the "Greenas," the greenhorns, the American way. Every day in class we were subjected to physical inspections. One day it might be for lice in our hair. The teacher actually went to each of us and poked a pencil in our hair, separating the follicles, checking out the scalp.

Another day it was our fingernails—they had to be clean. Or our shoes, which were to be shined. There were also the handkerchief inspections—each of us had to have one.

On the first day of school, we got our textbooks. On the second day of school we had to bring them in, covered with heavy-duty brown paper. These books had to last term to term. Every day we had to have two sharpened pencils, which sat in the furrow at the top of our desks. Next to it was the inkwell, which was filled daily for third-graders and above. Of course, if you used ink, then you had to use an ink-blotter to dry what you had written. When ballpoint pens came out, we weren't permitted to use them in class. They used to leak, or skip. And anyway, what kind of proper writing instrument was a pen without a point, without ink?

Patriotism was part of our daily life, so it was no huge leap of faith to get home in the afternoon to hear our heroes battling bad guys at home and abroad.

Every day in class started with the Pledge of Allegiance and singing the National Anthem. In assembly, every Friday, a student would read from the Bible. By the time I got to the sixth grade—a senior in grade school—I was asked to read to the assembled, and it was always the same—the Twenty-third Psalm, starting, "The Lord is my shepherd." We then sang "America the Beautiful," and I always tried to figure out the meaning of "amber waves of grain," and "purple mountains' majesty" and "fruited plain," and what God's "grace" was.

Although most of school was Jewish, we thought nothing of singing Christmas songs. Where else would I have learned "Silent Night?" What did "round yon Virgin" mean? Who knew? It was sing-able. As was "O Come, All Ye Faithful." So I sang the phrase "Let us adore Him," but never thought of Him as my God, merely as someone in a song I was singing.

In assembly, I also learned the words to the Chinese national anthem, called "Qilai!" which means "Arise!" I know the words still ("Arise! Ye who refuse to be slaves! . . ."). And we learned the United Nations anthem ("United Nations on the march, with flags unfurled . . .").

Oh, there was a sop to our Jewishness. On Chanukah we sang the "Chanukah Song," about the candles burning brightly. But that was about it. Jewish history, per se, was not taught, nor did I learn anything about the holidays—other than the fact we didn't have to go to school on those days. Jewish History Month? Who would have thought of it?

Rather than celebrate cultural differences, we were actually brought into the larger culture. This was the mission of many of our teachers who probably were not as well-educated as my generation was to be, and who had attended two-year "normal" schools and, who, invariably, seemed to be old maids with their hair tied into a bun.

But they knew how to teach us what we had to learn—and they sent us out to the larger world of junior high school knowing our "times tables," our Christmas songs, our classical music (well, the themes, at least). And we learned how important it was to have polished shoes, clean nails, a head free of lice, a handkerchief in our pocket, a sharpened pencil.

School was a somewhat less exciting counterpoint to radio life. It wasn't about exciting the kids of eleven, twelve, thirteen, or even in high school. Teachers weren't concerned about making us happy while we were learning. Their mission was to give us information. It was about studying and repetition. So just as I learned the multiplication tables by rote, without a calculator, I was forced to know dates when I was in the fifth grade. Imagine—we had to memorize Civil War dates, Civil War battles. Or the names of World War I cities. They told us when Vasco da Gama sailed for Africa from Portugal. When the Magna Carta was signed. How Verrazzano spelled his name and when he sailed. It was especially important to learn the history of New York City, of Peter Stuyvesant and Peter Minuet and Henry Hudson. We learned the name of Hudson's ship (the *Half Moon*). It's stuff that seems made for a trivia quiz today, but it was a major part of our education then. Every school child in New York was given a report-card grade in "citizenship" and "civics." I never quite knew what those meant. Penmanship mattered, as did the margins you kept on a sheet of paper. No one ever handed in a typewritten paper—even if you had a typewriter. For writing in long-hand was part of the assignment. If you typed, in a sense you'd be cheating, for then your penmanship would not be tested as well.

By the time we got to the sixth or seventh grades, we were expected to know about "our neighbors to the south" in Latin America, what their exports were, the names of the capital cities, the distances to them from New York. Thus, we learned about Simón Bolívar, and the Alamo, and the conquistadors. Our teachers taught us about the Inca and gold. Of course, we learned the simplistic stereotypes as well, and so Brazil meant coffee and Argentina meant gauchos and Mexico meant serapes and siestas. Yes, these generalizations dehumanized the people we read about;

they were cardboard characters, especially two-dimensional to me because I had never met or even seen one. The rise of Puerto Rican emigration to New York still was years away. And while California and Texas, for example, always had an ample percentage of Mexican Americans, the Latin influence on those of us growing up in the borough of Brooklyn, with its more than two million people, was negligible. While we might have received a smattering of information about the rest of the world, we learned little about Americans of African descent—those who had been slaves, and its impact on America. Oh, in grade school we knew of Lincoln, but it wasn't until later we learned of the abolitionists and the Underground Railroad and Harriet Beecher Stowe. When I was eleven or twelve years old, the only black man I read about was George Washington Carver, who, we were taught, invented dozens of uses for the peanut. In other words, what we knew of African American history was frivolous. Then again, they didn't teach us much about Jews, either. But by the time we got to junior high school we learned of Paul Robeson and Marion Anderson. By then, Jackie Robinson, who broke in with the Dodgers in 1947, when I was in the fifth grade, had become the one black person we spoke about in "current events."

Within two hours of the end of school, our good-citizenship ethos was reinforced further by our radio shows, which brought us into the world of good guys and bad guys, and often deputized us onto the side of law and order with our badges and rings and secret handshakes.

And, of course, we learned, by osmosis, some of the great themes of music. One of my favorite programs was a weekly show about the newspaper business called *The Big Story*, sponsored by Pall Mall cigarettes. It dramatized a true-life major newspaper story each week, focusing on the reporter and how the piece came about. The theme music was Richard Strauss's "Ein Heldenlaben."

Even outer-space fantasies, such as Buck Rogers, had the classics. His was Liszt's "Les Preludes." Captain Midnight, of course, weighed in with Wagner's "Flying Dutchman Overture," while Orson Welles's Mercury Theatre played Tchaikovsky's Piano Concerto No. 1. Meanwhile, the scary show *Escape* had the eerie "Night on Bald Mountain." *The Shadow* showed his intellectual side with "Omphales Spinning Wheel" (Opus 31), by Saint-Saëns.

Which brings me back to the Lone Ranger. He was my champion. Today, though, it is illegal in many states to walk around with a mask on.

The show was different from virtually every other kids' serial. The Lone Ranger was on for half an hour—three times a week. In New York, it was on WJZ, at 7:30 at night.

When the announcer introduced that night's show by saying, "Return with us now, to those thrilling days of yesteryear . . . the Lone Ranger rides again!" and was accompanied by tense orchestral strains, I immediately was transported back to the Old West, to the American myth of who we are and how we became, to the world of good and evil.

The Lone Ranger had not always been a loner. He was in a band of Texas Rangers that included his older brother, Daniel. But the troupe was ambushed by Butch Cavendish's scurrilous gang, and all were left for dead. All perished except one lone ranger, whose first name may have been "John." No one is quite certain. But "John" Reid was found in the carnage by the kindly Tonto, who revived him and then nursed him along.

But the Lone Ranger now was on a mission: to capture bad guys everywhere. He cut out part of the vest his dead brother had been wearing—it had two bullet holes in it. Then young Reid took a piece of the vest and wrapped it around his face—and where the bullet holes had been, he now could see through. He had his black mask.

As he and Tonto got up and about, they spied a white stallion. The ranger captured the stallion, which he named Silver. Then, another lucky find: a deserted silver mine. Some older listeners believe that he was bequeathed the mine by his brother. In any event, the ranger and Tonto also came across an old prospector and gave him a job—to make silver bullets out of the ore.

But the ranger also vowed that he never would shoot to kill—just to stop bad buys in their tracks. Oh, there was one killing over the years. He dispatched Butch Cavendish eventually.

And so went my Mondays, Wednesdays, and Fridays at 7:30:

A fiery horse with the speed of light, a cloud of dust, and a hearty "Hi-Yo, Silver!" The Lone Ranger. With his faithful Indian companion Tonto, the daring and resourceful masked rider of the Plains led the fight for law and order in the early western United States. Nowhere in the pages of history can one find a greater champion for justice. Return with us now to those thrilling days of yesteryear. From out of the past come the thundering hoofbeats of the great horse Silver. The Lone Ranger rides again!

How many crimes do any of us come across? But somehow, in the middle of the sagebrush, the Lone Ranger always found a poor soul who had just been ravaged, or heard about an awful event in the nearby town that remained unsolved. I never questioned how or why he came to be drawn to these situations. They just happened. And his character was his destiny, to make things right.

Announcer: Early one morning, the Lone Ranger's Indian friend Tonto rode into the town of Tobacco Ridge to buy supplies. When he returned to the masked man's camp, he reported:

> Tonto: There's plenty of excitement in town, kemosabe!
> Lone Ranger: Oh?
> Tonto: Crooks try to rob bank last night.
> Lone Rangers: Have Bogus Brown and his pal Elk been in town?
> Tonto: Umm. Them the fellers try to rob bank.
> Lone Ranger: Are you sure, Tonto?
> Tonto: Umm. Watchman get a good look at crooks in lantern light. And me hear description he give.

So they were off again.

Sky King hopped in his airplane, and also made use of short-wave radio, to bring the baddies to justice. This was true soaring adventure, and I pictured myself side-by-side at the controls in the cockpit.

Sky King personified how technology could bring to heel the world's bad boys—as if the simple act of flying a plane was somehow tied to crime-solving. Yet, about two dozen of these shows made it to the airwaves in the 1930s and 1940s.

The show was created by a pair of former World War I fighter pilots, but was a peacetime drama—indeed, it was launched a little more than a year after World War II ended. The same duo had created Captain Midnight, but Sky King was a little more prosaic, even though his title was quite royal. In fact, ads for the show depicted Sky King wearing a Western-style Stetson hat.

In reality, he was Schuyler J. King, a rancher in rural Grover City, Arizona. His spread was called the Flying Crown Ranch, and he flew a twin-engine Cessna called the *Songbird*. He was abetted by his niece and nephew, Penny and Clipper. To add to his cachet, during World War II he had been a naval aviator. The thugs never outran my hero.

Peter Pan peanut butter sponsored the show. One of the announcers was a young fellow named Myron Wallace, who soon changed his first name to Mike. Like the other shows, this had many premiums—my favorite was the serious-sounding Signalscope. It had a whistle, a magnifying glass, and a code-breaker. It was must-have, if you were going to be saving civilization as we knew it.

✳

Superman was played by Clayton Collyer, who was known as "Bud Collyer" when he hosted several television game shows, including *Beat the Clock*. In most Superman episodes, some bad person discovered a cache of kryptonite that temporarily immobilized the man from Krypton. These were awful moments for all us listeners as well. I was always frustrated because I knew where the poisonous kryptonite was hidden, but couldn't warn him.

That was part of the charm and the lure of Superman for me, and for all I know, for children everywhere. He was vulnerable, despite being the strongest man on Planet Earth.

I suppose that if you didn't have a conflict in a serial, you didn't have a serial. If the Man of Steel was impervious to everything, then what's the story? Even great Greek heroes flew too close to the sun; even Shakespeare's kings overreached or couldn't overcome family squabbles; even Mary Tyler Moore was forced to move on her own to Minneapolis after the live-in boyfriend she helped put through medical school left her.

So even though I knew of Superman's fabulous powers, I always was a bit nervous when some new character was introduced: Did this person have a stash of kryptonite in his suitcase? Was he a secret agent plotting the overthrow of civilization? The sense of vulnerability—mine?—was palpable, even for my Superman.

"Faster than an airplane. More powerful than a locomotive. Impervious to bullets," began the introduction. And then the excitement built as I heard the following:

> Up in the sky—look!
> It's a giant bird!
> It's a plane!
> It's Superman!

We memorized the opening—I can say it still. So can everyone my age. This dramatic beginning was followed by a brief explication of how Superman got here:

> And now—Superman, being no larger than an ordinary man, but possessed of powers and abilities never before recognized on Earth: able to leap into the air an eighth of a mile at a single bound, hurtle a twenty-story building with ease, race a high-powered bullet to its target, lift tremendous weights and rend solid steel in his bare hands as though it were paper. Superman, a strange visitor from a distant planet; champion of the oppressed, physical marvel extraordinary who has sworn to devote his existence on earth to helping those in need.

Collyer had remarkable voice control, and if you had heard him miraculously shift his persona, you would be impressed. At the moment he needed his great powers, you heard his Clark Kent voice say, in a tenor: "This is a job . . ." and then, an instant later, "for Superman!" in a lower register that might have been another actor's voice, for all I knew then.

He hooked up with Lois Lane early in the series, when she was working on a story about a stolen atomic ray gun. Lois was a smart, crafty veteran reporter who wished Clark could be more like Superman. Sometimes, it seemed, she almost had it figured out. She had suspicions about Clark's connections to the Man of Steel—why he always was around just before and after Superman got there—but she never made the leap of faith it took to put the two together.

Superman's other sidekick was cub reporter Jimmy Olsen, a post-teen character whose gee-whiz approach resonated with young people, I'm sure. The trio's gruff boss at the "Daily Planet" was city editor Perry White, who was forever badgering poor Clark about why Lois often got closer to the Superman story.

The greatest challenge Superman faced, in addition to shards of kryptonite—from his native planet Krypton—was the Atom Man. This creature was infused with kryptonite and presented an ever-present danger to the Man of Steel.

The Atom Man was played by the late Mason Adams, the well-known voice of "Pepper Young" and Smucker's jams—and who I met decades later as the neighbor of my cousins, Phyllis and Arthur Wachtel, who lived on Long Island Sound in Westport, Connecticut. Adams was a gracious, friendly guy—in whose veins, obviously, coursed something other than kryptonite.

Well, now that I'd met Mason, I thought it would be neat to talk to him about those long-ago radio days. So I visited him and Margot at their Park Avenue apartment one morning. He was eighty-five years old and sitting upright in a wheelchair, but he couldn't wait to get started talking. He was feisty and animated, and asked me to edit out all the colorful adjectives that dot his recollections.

"We had an ironclad rule on *Superman* that no one would be allowed in the clients' booth," said Adams, "and certainly no one under the age of twelve. We didn't want to destroy the illusion."

But during one episode, a youngster did in fact turn out. When the show was over, Adams headed for the elevator with the rest of the cast. "The young kid is at the elevator, too, and turns to his father and says in an awestruck whisper, pointing to me, 'See that little skinny guy with the eyeglasses—that's the Atomic Man!'"

Adams had what might be described as a cheerful voice, but to get the Atom Man just right, he said, "He had to have a deep, gravelly voice. On radio, it was all voice—voice carried characterization."

Precisely. Hearing was the only one of our senses for listeners of radio, and the voice we heard had to be everything about that character.

As for Superman—well, Adams was no fan of Collyer's. "As phony as a three-dollar bill," Mason said of the actor. "He was a reactionary so-and-so. He led the blacklist of actors during the anti-Communist hysteria."

Adams's role as Atom Man was one of the longest of his career, but he also had the lead on *Pepper Young's Family,* replacing Burgess Meredith, and there was a ten-year stint on *Grand Central Station,* from announcing the classic introduction to a variety of acting roles. He appeared with such landmark performers as Richard Widmark and Jason Robards.

On television, Adams also was Ed Asner's newsroom boss on *Lou Grant,* and he was the basketball coach on Broadway's *Tall Story.* One of his oldest friends was a producer who had been legendary on radio for the quality of his shows, but also was known as a penny-pincher. When the producer turned to television, expenses were even greater.

"Once we were doing a show that had a scene in a funeral parlor," recalled Adams. "It called for flowers in the place. So my friend happened to be passing a funeral in Brooklyn. He waited until everybody left, then went into the parlor and hauled out a bunch of flowers, which he put onto the set. I guess you could call him compulsively parsimonious."

Margot, his wife, remembered that Mason also was on a score of soap operas, which was daily fare for "housewives" of the 1940s and 1950s. "Sometimes we'd meet women who weren't about to admit they did housework," said Margot, "and they'd tell us, 'Our maid always used to listen to you.'"

However, I'm not ashamed to admit I did, too.

Before Atom Man, Superman still faced the ever-present danger of kryptonite in other forms. As the deep-voiced announcer, Jackson Beck, once explained, "Superman for the first time in his life faces an enemy against which he is entirely powerless. That enemy is a piece of the planet Krypton—kryptonite, it is called—which a few days ago struck the Earth in the form of a meteor. A full understanding of his danger came to Superman when he approached the kryptonite for the first time. As he came within five feet of the mass of metal, which glowed like a green diamond, he suddenly felt weak, as if all his strength had been drained from him."

⁂

When the war ended, Superman had to find antagonists other than those who would destroy the world. In one famous episode, he actually saved a rabbi and a Catholic priest who had founded Unity House, a place where diverse religions lived in harmony. When some very bad people—gang members under the influence of a former spy—tried to destroy Unity House, Superman took over. After he restored law and order, he addressed the wayward gang:

"Remember this as long as you live: Whenever you meet up with anyone who is trying to cause trouble between people—anyone who tries to tell you that a man can't be a good citizen because of his religious beliefs—you can be sure that troublemaker is a rotten citizen himself and an inhuman being. Don't ever forget that."

A few weeks after the Japanese surrendered, it was apparent that Superman's energies would have to go in a different direction—in retrospect, a bizarre direction. On the lookout for danger, or on his daily rounds as a good Samaritan, Superman flew over a rowboat adrift at sea. There was a young boy in it, unconscious. Of course, Superman could see through the youngster's clothing—the X-ray vision thing—and clear as day was a letter "R" on a red vest under the boy's shirt.

"Great Scott!" said Superman. "If this boy is who I think it is, this is serious business." And it was, for that boy was none other than Robin— Batman's sidekick. Less than a week later, Superman also rescued Batman, helping forge a bond among the trio.

I think that by the time I was nine years old, I figured it out that Superman was somewhat less than real. But listening to him, I still wondered how he'd use his fabulous powers to save someone—after all, who could hide from him? Yet, they managed to find a way. But when Superman caught the evil-doers, he never killed them. In fact, he never did more than throw a restraining poke, despite being the Man of Steel. He was a compassionate pseudo-lawman who never used his great gifts to show off, merely to overpower evil.

I wore Superman pajamas with pride, and remember—I don't know how accurately—dreaming of being able to jump off buildings and fly.

∗

Captain Midnight, with the help of his Secret Squadron that included two young associates, helped foil Ivan Shark and his dyspeptic daughter, Fury. He was always in danger, as opposed to some of my other heroes who were on the outside looking in, attempting to solve crimes.

Once again, the good captain was empowered to fight crime because he was using the most modern instrument: an airplane. What good, really, did an airplane do in solving espionage? Or trapping someone who would bring down these United States? Nothing, really. You might as well create a detective story on television today with the guy using his laptop computer as a secret weapon. But anyone using an airplane instantly had cachet in my imagination. The plane gave Midnight a magical aura, just like, say, a ring with a tiny hidden compartment would enable me to hide secrets (very small secrets) in case I were captured by . . . whom, exactly? Well, it probably would have been someone with a strange, ominous accent.

Like so many of these extraordinary good guys, the captain had a sidekick. His was the mechanic Ichabod (Icky) Mudd. The name itself connoted goofiness and allowed a leit motif of humor when Mudd was involved. The more serious work was done by Chuck Ramsey and Joyce Ryan, the key members of the Secret Squadron.

Young Chuck often used the "Code-O-graph" to contact a mysterious "Major Steele" in Washington to extricate the trio from a threatening situation. And of course, Captain Midnight had the trappings of modernity, including a "gliderchute," something like a parasailing contraption that allowed him to glide over hard-to-find places. One of his weapons was a doom beam torch.

The captain's real name was Jim (Red) Albright, whose feud with Shark had started long before—back in World War I, when they had met in dogfights over Europe. Albright, of course, was in the Air Corps while Shark flew for the Hun, as the Germans often were derisively called. Albright then piloted cargo planes when the Great War ended. But he was actually an undercover agent for an unspecified agency in Washington that battled espionage and other bad things.

Ivan Shark kept all of Washington busy. He was forever stealing the plans for a newfangled weapon that was sure to tip the balance of power in favor of an enemy country. Midnight had to get the weapon, or the plans for the weapon, back. Often, Shark kidnapped the scientist who invented this new demonic device.

By the time I began listening, Midnight was sponsored by Ovaltine. It was one of the most felicitous pairings of food with crime-fighting in all of radio, rivaling the Jack Armstrong–Wheaties connection, or the one between Superman and Kellogg's Pep. I don't remember that Captain Midnight's initial sponsor was the Skelly Oil Company, which described itself as the "originator of tailor-made gasoline," and actually advised boys and girls to tell their dads about Skelly's wonders for their car.

In the cauldron of World War II, Captain Midnight came alive. While today's children vaporize all the bad guys on electronic hand-held machines, our connection to our radio heroes was more intellectual. I never shot anyone. We were part of the fact-finding sleuths who helped crack these mysterious cases. Thus, the Sliding Compartment Ring, ideal for hiding a sliver of microfilm. I did not, however, know any ten-year-olds who owned a microfilm camera, so it was of little use to me. But I could use the Mystic Eye Detector Ring. It had a stainless-steel mirror. If you held it right next to your eye, you could see who was sneaking up behind you. And always, we were on the lookout, or listening, for enemy planes. To help us, Ovaltine sold us the MJC-10 Plane Spotter, which displayed airplane silhouettes—"ours" and "theirs."

Closer at hand, there was a Magni-Magic Code-O-Graph. The center of this badge had an extremely important crime-fighting and life-saving tool—a magnifying glass. Ovaltine hawked the Spy Scope.

Invariably, one of these tricky little items was used by the captain, or his junior assistants, and then quickly were available for purchase. What drove your desire to buy Ovaltine was hardly its taste, but the goodies you got by sending in the lid. It probably was the all-time champion in this regard.

A typical ending:

> What can Captain Midnight do now? His plane is hopelessly mired in the dried lake and he and his friends seem to be at Ivan Shark's mercy. Or are they? Be sure to listen, tomorrow.
>
> Until then, this is Don Gordon, your Skelly man, saying good-bye and . . .
> GONG UP
> . . . Happy Landings!
> GONG CONTINUES AND PLANE UP THEN ALL FADE

Hop Harrigan, a pilot who leaped to fame just as air power was born during World War II, was "America's ace of the airways," assisted, of course, by his sidekick mechanic, Tank Tinker.

It was one of two dozen shows reaching back to the 1920s—spurred by Charles Lindbergh's solo hop across the Atlantic—that featured aviation. They had names such as *Wings of Destiny*, and *Speed Gibson of the International Secret Police*.

Hop spent World War II chasing enemies. One of the shows, in fact, was called "Trapped in Mine by Japs."

Before the episode began, the announcer would tell a real-life story of a heroic pilot, and end the tidbit with "America needs flyers!"

How could I become one? I wondered. While this show failed to insinuate itself into the consciousness of youngsters the way *Captain Midnight* did, it kept up the fantasy that somehow a preteen could help out his country. I know I was ready to serve.

✳

Tom Mix, the cinema cowboy who allowed his name to be used (he never actually appeared on the radio show), had an eclectic series of enemies—they ranged from ghosts to cattle rustlers. I enjoyed the no-frills way he went about his business.

By the time the radio serials were in their heyday, Mix had already died—his luxury car had gone off the road in 1940 (his horse Tony died two years later, to the day). But Ralston, with its famed checkerboard-square logo and address, adopted him as its own, and he probably was associated with a product more strongly than any character except Jack Armstrong with Wheaties.

Legends—his own and his publicist's—followed the Tom Mix story even after his death. Born in Pennsylvania, he claimed to have had an earlier career fighting with Teddy Roosevelt's Rough Riders, had been a U.S. marshal, had been wounded in the Philippines. Supposedly, trying to make ends meet in the 1930s—he was married five times—after being one of Hollywood's highest-paid silent-screen stars, he signed an agreement on the back of an envelope with Ralston. It permitted the cereal-maker to use his name, but no one expected a Tom Mix show to become so wildly popular.

The perennial role of hero sidekick was called "The Old Wrangler" (who rode Calico). The juveniles were named "Jane" and "Jimmy," both Mix's wards. They operated out of the TM Bar Ranch.

And while there was the usual assortment of rustlers, the show also had science-fiction overtones, with ghost riders and mysterious caves. Somehow, Mix also wound up fighting for the Allies in Europe in some episodes during the war. But these shows, alas, did not have his spirited steed, Tony.

I was, naturally, a member of the Straight Shooters club, which meant I knew the secret handshake and a secret password. I bought one of the whistling rings, and even sprang for the invisible ink offer.

※

Jack Armstrong taught me about America—at least, the America outside my Brooklyn borders.

He went to Hudson High, and his buddies were Billy and Betty Fairfield. Who among us in East New York, Brooklyn, with its million immigrants, had names like that?

The show was similar to *Midnight* for premiums—many were tied in with the storyline. There was a dragon's-eye ring, for example, that figured in the plot while Jack was doing undercover work in the Philippines.

Of course, he had a signature opening, one that got my blood flowing, pumped me up for what was coming—something like a fight song.

"Jack Armstrong . . . Jack Armstrong. . . . Jack Armstrong! The All-American Boy!"

Then the school song, not quite as classical as, say, the Green Hornet's "Flight of the Bumblebee" or the Lone Ranger's "William Tell Overture." This one went:

> Wave the flag for Hudson High, boys
> Show them how we stand,
> Ever shall our team be champions,
> Known throughout the Land

Jack and the Fairfield kids, whose Uncle Jim usually led their expeditions, often took strange excursions: such as taking a dirigible to India. Another show was called "Easter Island Adventure," and another was "Country of the Head-Hunters." This was serious travel, with serious dangers.

Brilliantly, the gadgets and amulets that Jack used on the show were hawked incessantly. Even a pedometer figured in Jack's life. That little contraption, of course, was essential when he had to follow step-by-step the exact directions to avoid the bottomless pit in an episode involving the feared Cult of the Crocodile God.

> Announcer: . . . Today, Jack Armstrong starts on a brand new radio adventure. One of the most exciting and dangerous he's ever had! I know you won't want to miss a single episode of this thrilling Jack Armstrong adventure. In the second place, we're welcoming back a lot of Jack Armstrong's old friends. . . . We hope that you'll get a lot of thrills and real pleasure out of Jack Armstrong's newest adventure, and that you'll make the acquaintance of those extra good Wheaties flakes right away. You know, right now, at the very beginning of a new school year. . . . So, would you do this for me? Would you eat a Breakfast of Champions the next four mornings in a row. Then ask yourself if you've ever found any other breakfast dish that gives you as much real pleasure and satisfaction. . . . And now, Jack Armstrong . . . the All-American Boy!
>
> Announcer: After their thrilling experiences on Easter Island, Jack, Betty, and Billy. . . .

Mark Trail, a forest ranger for the ages, had all sorts of hazardous jobs, including, as the show announced each week, "battling the raging elements." His show episodes had titles such as "The Witch of Lost Forest." His adventures took him into the great outdoors—very far from my Brooklyn.

In the original comic strip the show was based on, Mark Trail always had a pipe jutting out of his mouth, and his hair was black and shiny and groomed with a brilliant sheen—but he always had a lock just curling down onto his forehead. Sort of showing his outdoorsiness, I'd guess. He was a conservationist, animal-lover, and ecologist before any of us ever had heard of that word.

*

Of course, there were other shows—dozens during my listening years: *Sergeant Preston of the Yukon,* whose dog, King, would punctuate the end of each show with an affirmative "woof" after Preston, the Royal Canadian Mountie, would tell him, "Well, King, it looks as if this job is finished!" *Dick Tracy* and his cast of characters who included one villain who had no chin. *Terry and the Pirates,* battling scurvy sorts in Asian countries or the high seas. His favorite villain(ess) was the Dragon Lady.

But my daily dose (and, for the Lone Ranger, three times a week) included the others. Like Sergeant Preston's signature sign-off, virtually all my shows had some comforting repeated phrase, either in the story or intoned by an announcer. The Lone Ranger always got his horse Silver ready by exhorting, "Up, big fella!" while the Green Hornet invariably commanded his valet, "Get the car, Kato," and Hop Harrigan was ready for a landing by telling the control tower, "OK, this is Hop Harrigan coming in."

The weekend set a different tone for me, with its self-contained dramas. No waiting two days to see how your cliffhanger comes out. These were half-hour shows, starting Saturday mornings with *Let's Pretend.*

*

The Green Hornet, who actually was the Lone Ranger's great-nephew (I never knew that until I started doing some research), was also a newspaper publisher with aspirations to be a super-hero; he took off in his souped-up car to foil those who would sully his city. The theme music was "The Flight of the Bumble Bee." I think the newspaper aspect attracted me, as well as his ability to morph.

Britt Reid was the publisher of the *Daily Sentinel.* When he turned into the Green Hornet, he never actually killed the bad guys. He had what might whimsically be called a stun gun—it fired knockout gas. Reid never told the police about his other identity. Indeed, often he would disguise himself as a crook, infiltrating a thieves' nest, and then take them all down. Then, invariably, he would call the police—leaving the scene just before they arrived.

How did Reid know about all these underworld hi-jinks? He often was tipped off because of his newspaper position—another fantasy of an earlier era. As if reporters (or publishers) were the first people a crook or an associate would call when he got word of an impending crime.

The opening was typically breathless, capturing my attention from the first buzz:

Announcer: The Green Hornet!

F/X [Special Effects]: Hornet buzz

Announcer: He hunts the biggest of all game—public enemies that try to destroy our America.

Music (Flight of the Bumblebee) up and under

Announcer: With his faithful valet, Kato, Britt Reid, daring young publisher, matches wits with racketeers and saboteurs. Risking his life that criminals and enemy spies will feel the weight of the law by the sting of the Green Hornet.

F/X: Black Beauty races off

Announcer: Ride with Britt Reid in the thrilling adventure, "The Corpse That Wasn't There." The Green Hornet strikes again!

F/X: Hornet buzz

Music up and then fade under announcer.

Announcer: Miss Case and Ed Lowry were returning to the *Daily Sentinel* after lunch. The streets were crowded and as they took their last corner, a man hurrying from the opposite direction ran into them.

All three: Oh. Ah.

Man: Excuse me, I'm in a hurry.

Lowry: Hey, why don't you watch where you're goin' you . . . I tell you Casey, sometimes I think they need traffic lights on the sidewalk, too. You OK?

Case: Yes. Except for my handbag.

Lowry: Um. Oh, wait, here it is on the sidewalk. Hey, this yours too?

Case: What?

Lowry: This letter.

Case: No, it's not mine. It . . . it's already been mailed hasn't it?

Lowry: Yeah. Mailed and unsealed. Hum.

Case: Uh-oh, Lowry, never mind your reporter instincts. It's not right to look at other people's mail.

Lowry: Nuts, I wasn't going to open it. Well, what do we do with it? Throw it away?

Case: It may be important . . .

And so it began. This particular show was called "The Corpse That Wasn't There," and ended this way:

Newsboy: Extree! Extree! Murder mystery spy tells all! Read all about it. Green Hornet still at large. Extree! Extree!

Music Up

Announcer: You have just heard the adventure, "The Corpse That Wasn't There." These exciting adventures are sent to you each week at this same time. . . .

The Shadow, once played by Orson Welles, scared me when he took on his secret persona. The music would be eerie, and he would also frighten the bad guys with a secret he learned in the Orient—"the hypnotic power to cloud men's minds so they cannot see him."

Usually, the Shadow was Lamont Cranston, "wealthy young man about town." But when he turned invisible, his voice changed as well. It became nasal, higher, and mysterious.

This was a perfect show for me—he was invisible, and it was radio, so he was somewhere out there in the ether, for me and for the bad guys. We were literally experiencing him at the same time.

"Who knows what evil l-l-lurks in the hearts of men?" he asked at the show's opening, rolling the "l." Then he would laugh—malevolently—as he answered his own question: "The shadow does!" This laugh was so distinctive that Welles himself couldn't pull it off. Instead, the show used another actor's voice for the laugh.

The sponsor was Blue Coal—that's right, coal had brand names back then, and it was the fuel of choice for Americans. Like most families in the neighborhood, we burned coal. We actually had a coal cellar on the side of our house. Once a week, the coal truck would pull up to the side of the house, some thickly muscled guy in an undershirt would roll a wooden barrel to the rear of the truck, open the chute, and the coal tumbled out in a cloud of gray dust. Then he rolled the barrel to the side of the cellar, placed a ramp over the opening, and turned the barrel on its side. He poured half a ton of coal into that cellar weekly.

The Shadow had no comic sidekick. Instead his companion, Margo Lane—the only person who knew his secret—was swept along his crime-fighting path. When Orson Welles, a twenty-two-year-old, performed the Shadow in the late 1930s, Ms. Lane was played by a member of his acting troupe, Agnes Moorehead. She was part of Welles's remarkable entourage at the Mercury Theatre of the Air, which he founded as the Mercury Theatre with John Houseman.

The titles of *The Shadow* sound so campy today, you would think they were a put-on. But that's how send-ups start: in reality. Thus, we had "The Society of the Living Dead," and "The Devil Takes a Wife."

✳

"The weed of crime bears bitter fruit. Crime does not pay," the Shadow intoned each week.

There was something almost Sunday-schoolish about this admonition, as if all of us listening had it in us to be bad, but were scared into being good. A simpler time? To say the least. But no less real. At least, to me.

> Blue Coal presents The Shadow, the mystery man who strikes terror into the very hearts of sharpsters, lawbreakers, and criminals. Today: The Death Triangle.
>
> Music.
>
> People murmuring.
>
> Drum roll.
>
> Voice: On this day, December 22, 1913, by order of the authority of Devil's Island, you, Pierre Martan, are hereby sentenced to one hundred days in confinement solitaire.
>
> Men's murmuring.
>
> Voice: And one hundred lashes in the presence of the assembled prisoners, as a warning to all would attempt to escape. Let the punishment begin.
>
> Drum Roll.
>
> Martan: I will find the devil who betrayed me.
>
> Voice: One!
>
> Sound of lash.
>
> Martan: I will learn his name.

Voice: Two!
Martan: I will kill him . . .

Another Shadow show had this portentous and, to me, annoying
beginning. For everyone in the Shadow's hometown seemed to believe
he was a bad guy. How come kids like me knew he was a true hero and
the grown-ups didn't?

Music.
News Announcer: Ladies and gentlemen, we interrupt this program of
organ music to bring you a special newsflash. . . . The Shadow has been
found. Dr. James Evans, world-famous child surgeon, told reporters this
afternoon that a wounded man who claimed to be the Shadow forced his
way into Dr. Evans's private clinic, and at the point of a gun, forced him
to remove a bullet. The wounded man revealed that he was none other
than that mysterious character who waged a one-man war against crime,
the Shadow. Before Dr. Evans could report the case to the police, however, the Shadow mysteriously disappeared. The famous surgeon believes
the Shadow has little chance of surviving his wound. Our organ music
now continues . . .

This inversion also was a theme of many other shows in which my
fabulous heroes had secret identities: thus, the Lone Ranger, the Green
Hornet, even Superman and/or Batman often were mistaken for villains.
Why else would they wear a disguise?
Take this *Superman* segment, in which he and Batman and Robin have
at last found one another:

After disappearing mysteriously for almost two weeks, the famous
Batman apparently reappeared in the Metropolitan Auditorium, and
delivered a rabble-rousing un-American speech. Then, confronted by
Robin, his young companion, Batman struck the bewildered youngster,
knocking him out. A short time later, Robin, having been brought home
by Superman, received a telephone call, apparently from Batman, who
told him to come alone to a shady hotel on the waterfront, where he
would explain his strange actions, and when Robin arrived there, he
walked into an ambush. Meanwhile, unaware of this development,
Superman, disguised as reporter Clark Kent, was at the Opera House in
Willow Falls . . .

But radio also had a reality component mixed in with the fantasy. There were shows that made even me, as a preteen, involved in halting crime.

Gangbusters was a case in point. Supposedly produced "in cooperation with police and law enforcement departments throughout the United States," which made me feel I was listening to a quasi-governmental broadcast, it was the end of the show that I looked forward to. For after a fairly routine cops-and-robbers adventure, the announcer then broadcast the FBI's Ten Most Wanted list and a description of one of the wanted.

I had paper and pencil ready for the description of these folks, all of them "armed and dangerous" as we were told by the announcer. (One of the narrators was an official of the New Jersey State Police, H. Norman Schwarzkopf—yes, father of the Desert Storm commander, and who had some notoriety himself back in the early 1930s when he was a lead investigator in the Lindbergh baby kidnapping). Often, a "real-life" police officer was enlisted to tell that night's story. However, the term "by proxy" was used in introducing this "real" person, meaning that an actor actually did the narration.

But the *Gangbusters* weekly search for the most wanted felons in America enlisted me and who knows how many thousands, if not millions, of amateur sleuths. We were on the lookout for guys with scars on their right cheek, or tattoos on their left arm, or someone who was bald and menacing. These were descriptions of real criminals, and updates on how many had been caught thanks to the successful suspicions of kids just like me.

"If you see this man," the announcer concluded after a description, "notify the FBI, your local law-enforcement agency, or *Gangbusters* at once!"

While the ending was dramatic and calculated to send you out after criminals, the beginning was noisy with police sirens and the staccato din of machine-gun fire.

Yes, you could actually be part of something bigger by listening to your radio—unlike, say, Jack Armstrong or Sky King, that you knew, deep down, wasn't real. Yet, when I think about it, the reality of *Gangbusters* was actually fantasy. That I could actually go out and find a criminal—a ten-year-old in a city of eight million—why, it would be easier to spot Superman leaping a tall building.

Still, there was another show: *The F.B.I. in Peace and War* also touched the edge of the real and the make-believe. Who could tell where one left off and the other began?

This one had a deeply sonorous theme—Prokofiev's "The Love of Three Oranges," and an equally lower-register commercial from Lava soap. A basso would sing only four notes—"L-A-V-A . . . L-A-V-A" accompanied by a gong as he blurted out each note. Lava was a heavy-duty "man's" soap—the kind that got rid of grit and grime. Another sponsor was Wildroot Cream Oil ("Get Wildroot Cream Oil, Charlie / Start using it today . . .")

Gangbusters mattered, I think, because in the mind of many Americans, fictional characters mixed with the real—the endless array of black-and-white film gangsters: James Cagney, Humphrey Bogart, Edward G. Robinson. How could I separate them from Al Capone, or Machine Gun Kelly, or Babyface Nelson, or Clyde Barrow? In a way, they were made heroic figures by newspapers and magazines, then turned into larger-than-life re-creations on the screen. Why, the Justice Department, years later, even paid homage to these silver-screen mobsters with its RICO statute. That is an anagram (Racketeer Influenced and Corrupt Organizations). However, the RICO film-goers remember was the Edward G. Robinson character named Rico in the movie *Little Caesar.* He is gunned down in the street, and his dying words are, "Mother of Mercy! Is this the end of Rico?" I think the Justice Department slyly stole the movie mobster's name.

Stories for *The F.B.I. in Peace and War*—how's that for covering all bases?—came, it was said, "from the files of the Federal Bureau of Investigation." However, the program never actually was authorized by the agency. It had an ongoing character (Field Agent Sheppard) who helped solve these weekly mysteries that had titles such as "The Fence," and "The Bungler."

Chapter 9

Good Humor

Kids laughed at grown-up jokes. There was no such delineation as "adult" comedy as there is today. Or a time of day to listen, only for grown-ups, or a rating only for adults. For the kinds of drama and humor we listened to on the radio was palatable enough for kids and grown-ups. My mother never was concerned—rightly—that I would pick up bad language, or evil thoughts, because I listened to Jack Benny, or Bob Hope, or Charlie McCarthy. There may have been children's drama, shows earmarked for us, but that didn't exclude us from listening to the mysteries for "grown-ups," and it certainly didn't stop us from listening to, and laughing at, the huge complement of comedians who had their own radio shows.

It is an odd, even incredible, conceit: a ventriloquist and his dummy on radio. Yet, every Sunday night, I listened to Edgar Bergen and Charlie McCarthy. Charlie's character was so well-defined and consistent that it hardly mattered he didn't really exist at all. Unlike ventriloquist acts on television that actually depended on the skill of the ventriloquist to disguise his lip movements, and that became almost as significant as the character of the dummy, Charlie was allowed to develop his own personality. He was a brash, back-talking wise guy, forever making fun of Bergen.

The actual name of the show was *The Chase and Sanborn Hour*, sponsored by that brand of coffee. Charlie, we knew from his picture in the newspapers, wore a monocle and a top hat. He was a leering teenager, or child, or post-teen. It was hard to tell which. But he was able to get away with double-entendres because he was, after all, a dummy. Thus, he bantered with Mae West, who told him, "Come up and see me sometime."

"What would I do?" asked Charlie.

"Maybe I'll let you play in my woodpile," West responded, a reply that made radio history for its sexiness.

Charlie had a running gag with W. C. Fields, a frequent guest, who always spoke of Charlie's wooden ancestry while the dummy always had a riposte involving Fields's drinking:

Fields: "Is it true your father was a table?"

Charlie: "Well, if it is, your father was under it."

I enjoyed his sidekick, Mortimer Snerd, as much. Mortimer sounded dumb and, when I finally saw him on television, I wasn't disappointed. He was dressed like a hayseed, and had outlandish buck teeth and hooded, half-closed eyelids that gave him a constantly befuddled expression.

Jack Benny (a guest on the show): "Mortimer, how did you get so stupid?"

Mortimer Snerd: "Well, I got a good deal and I couldn't turn it down."

The program was live, as were all the comedy shows. Audiences in person and on radio already knew the personalities of the characters and so we all laughed at the jokes as well as laughed at our own understanding of the character.

Thus, even at the age of seven or eight, I laughed at money jokes involving Jack Benny, whose character as a skinflint had been etched for years. Invariably, there'd be a money joke. Maybe he'd be going down to his vault—you'd hear creaking of a heavy metal door that sounded as if it hadn't been opened in years. We laughed. Or he'd have to go to his wallet for a dollar bill, and a moth would fly out.

Of course, his great gag, the one that people who monitor these sorts of things claim as evoking the longest sustained laughter in the history of radio, occurs as he is being robbed.

Crook: "Your money or your life."

Laughter, as Benny hesitates, then obviously looks to the audience for support.

After a long wait, as the audience's laughter grows louder with each passing second, the crook finally says, "Well?"

Benny replies, "I'm thinking it over."

The cast included the obese announcer, Don Wilson, a foil for Benny's cheapness; the valet, Rochester, who wisecracked his way past his boss's mercurial ways with money; Dennis Day, the singer and simpleton; the tippler band leader Phil Harris, and Mary Livingstone, Benny's real-life wife and radio (unmarried) partner who cynically put up with his foibles.

Bob Hope was a radio comic and a movie star at the same time. That was hardly unusual for what is now widely known as old-time radio. For movie and stage stars not only appeared in dramas, as noted earlier, but also thought nothing of being heard, even as regulars, on radio comedies. At least one, Don Ameche, even was an announcer. So I could hear W. C. Fields, or Frances Langford, or Jane Russell, or Jack Benny appear on other stars' shows. Bing Crosby showed up on Bob Hope's shows, as did Frank Sinatra—not to forget Cary Grant and Gary Cooper. Hope's show was the highest-rated on radio, and so celebrities flocked to the broadcast, especially if they had a movie about to debut.

I listened to Hope mostly between wars—World War II and Korea—when most of his radio shows revolved around his constant, failed attempts to impress a famous Hollywood beauty, especially the so-called sex symbols. The program was called *The Pepsodent Show*, and began with a monologue, often making fun of a national figure in politics or show business. Invariably, he broadcast from a military base, such as one from Greenland, where he quipped, "It was so cold here that a soldier fell out of bed and broke his pajamas."

I don't believe he actually said it, but Hope is credited with the following dialogue with Dorothy Lamour, whose claim to fame was the sarong she wore in the movies. She was always the perennial love interest for both Hope and Crosby in their "Road" movies (although "love" really wasn't what it was about; she often was the foil for their wrangling).

Supposedly, on the air, Lamour said to him, "Meet me at the pawn shop." To which Hope is said to have replied, "And kiss me under the balls." Again, I know of at least two people who claim to have heard that one—but since one of them is the same fellow who says he heard Uncle Don utter into an open mike, "That oughta hold the little bastards," I wondered whether this really happened. I called the world's great show-business trivia and history expert, Joe Franklin, about the notorious pawn shop dialogue.

"Nah, never happened," he said. "But I'll tell you what Hope did say that got him in trouble: 'Girls' skirts are going so high that they'll have to powder four cheeks.'"

And that was as raunchy as it got. Hope might have tried to slip in slightly nuanced sex, but never, ever a bad word. None of the comedy shows did. The closest you'd ever hear to a curse word would be a Charlie

McCarthy exclamation, "Why you . . . !" and then his voice would trail off, leaving the audience in stitches. For the audience knew what he was thinking, and in those days that was enough to elicit much more than a titter.

That really made us all part of the show, in a sense. Even as a child, I caught on to the Jack Benny or Bob Hope or Charlie McCarthy character, and character drove their shows. Character created a built-in response. If an actor asks another for a nickel to make a phone call, it's not funny. But ask Jack Benny for a nickel, and you knew instantly that the penny-pincher would say something that struck us as funny, because it involved money. Charlie couldn't leer, in person or on radio, but you knew what he was thinking when Lamour asked him for a kiss.

Similarly, *Fibber McGee and Molly* was as much about the humor in knowing how the characters would react as the story lines. So there was the weekly search at their home at 79 Wistful Vista for some obscure household item—an ironing cord, say. Molly would need one and Fibber—he came by his name because of outrageous fishing and hunting tales—would say he'd go looking for it in the hall closet. Molly would reply, "Nice to have known you, McGee," and the audience laughed as did I at home. Because I knew that he would open that dreaded closet and a lifetime's worth of junk would clamber out of it, rolling and clanking. And then, just to punctuate it, a cowbell would tinkle as the last item to fall out. In fact, "Fibber McGee's Closet" became a national byword for anything that was junk-filled.

The situations really didn't matter in *Fibber McGee and Molly,* or in another husband-and-wife broadcast such as *George Burns and Gracie Allen.* In the latter, it was Gracie's hare-brained observations and explanations and malaprops ("they're sending the prisoner to the hot plate"), always inspiring George's matter-of-fact replies of a spouse who knows that whatever he says it will not change her. World-weary, he says at the end of every show, "Say goodnight, Gracie," and she, of course, replies, "Goodnight, Gracie."

Dopey women and dopey men abounded in my radio world. Yes, there were stereotypes of silly women, and even dumb blondes, such as *My Friend Irma.* But McGee was the illogical one and not his wife, and even Ozzie had grand schemes that never panned out, no surprise to his wife, Harriet. Hope was sexist by today's standards, just a horny guy by those of his long era, while McCarthy was lecherous in a harmless way. The battle between the sexes never intruded on Jack Benny's world. He was not married on his radio show. Mary, his real-life wife, was there as part of a large cast. She was as much his girlfriend as anything else on the broadcast. Supposedly, he had met her at a department store, where she sold lingerie. Thus, every time he mentioned the May Department Store, the audience laughed. Quite sexy, no?

Chapter 10

Why I Drank That Horrible Ovaltine

Box tops were part of growing up, once upon a time. I had a third-grade teacher, Mrs. Miller, who spent the better part of her teaching career collecting Maltex cereal box tops. Someone had once told her that if you collected enough of them, you could get a set of the *Encyclopaedia Britannica.*

I never heard of Maltex, but I made my grandmother buy two boxes. On the front of the box it read, "Will not lump in cooking." I ate it once, then never again. But I removed the box top, leaving it vulnerable to the ants and roaches that were part of our extended family. (We had no plastic containers back then, or plastic wrap.) One opened box without a top was bad enough, but my grandmother was perplexed when the second box, which was otherwise untouched, also had a missing top. I think the Maltex myth was similar to the one about saving silver foil. Once you got a four-foot ball of it, then what?

All I know is that three years later, when I was graduating from the sixth grade, Mrs. Miller still didn't have her *Britannica,* but her kids still were snipping off the tops of that dry-as-crumbs cereal.

That era gave us a respect for knowledge and a simplistic view of intelligence—it was obtainable and would open all doors. And why not?

Above them all was the archaically spelled *Encyclopaedia Britannica.* All of us in the neighborhood had been subjected at some point to door-to-door salesmen hawking the big thing. I begged my mother for one when the guy came knocking. He showed us a beautifully bound volume, and he had statistics to show how much better kids who had the encyclopedia did in school (a marketing tool, by the way, also used by typewriter salesmen; of course, families with typewriters probably were from a higher socioeconomic class than those without them).

In any event, I knew of only one kid in the neighborhood who had the *Britannica:* a fat boy whose mother once complained that I was somewhat low-class because I asked to use their bathroom. I never actually saw the encyclopedia in his house until one day I dropped a penny while we were listening to the radio in his room. The penny rolled under the bed. I went there to get it—and saw the big cardboard box stuffed with the twenty-pound volume of books. So much for making you smarter. They had been suckered by a salesman. Perhaps they thought that merely keeping the books in the house conferred brilliance. After I became a reporter, the *Britannica* people called and asked if I'd write a section on "ice hockey." They were offering a ridiculously small amount of money, but I was able to get them to throw in a set of encyclopedias. When the huge carton arrived, I had visions of sticking it under my bed. But my wife, a teacher of the gifted, claimed she had no use for encyclopedias, that rather than inform they were the easy way out for kids, so I sold the set. Anyway, I'm glad I made some money on the deal. It made up for the insult from my fat friend's mother.

Britannica was the gold standard of intelligent research in my public school days, however. It was the prize offered if you could stop the experts on a quirky Tuesday night broadcast called *Information Please.* This was a quiz show with no one from the audience, but rather an eclectic panel that included John Kieran, the *New York Times* sports columnist; Oscar Levant, the manic pianist and great friend of the late George Gershwin; columnist Franklin P. Adams, and other intellectuals. There were guests from all over—Gracie Allen of Burns and Allen, Carl Sandburg, Orson Welles, Lillian Gish. Its enduring legacy is the *Information Please Almanac,* the annual compendium of facts ranging from world capitals to phases of the moon.

There was a joyousness to the intellectual bantering—I caught on to the wordplay and the love of language the panelists demonstrated.

There was a famous exchange between the moderator, Clifton Fadiman, and the author John Gunther that went something like this, after Gunther correctly identified the name of the Shah of Iran.

"Are you shah?" asked Fadiman.

"Sultanly," replied Gunther.

If you were lucky enough to have your question read, you'd get a fifty-dollar bond. If you stumped the experts, you could get an encyclopedia set. People sent in questions asking how many players on a lacrosse team, or to name the panelists' congressmen, or to quote a Shakespearean character.

I devoured this banter, and saw that a range of information didn't make you, in the word of the day, "a faggot." Back then, the connotation "faggot" had more to do with being a nerd than sexual orientation—especially if you weren't even ten years old. Amazing what information you learned when listening to *Information Please.*

Before there was *The $64,000 Question* on television, there was the sixty-four-dollar question on the radio show called *Take It or Leave It.* If you think the TV show got people excited—well, sixteen or thirty-two or sixty-four dollars back in the 1940s got people out of their seats.

This is how it began: You got a simple question for a dollar, then were given the choice of doubling it—that's right, your next answer was worth two dollars. If you took it, you kept going until you had the testosterone to try for sixty-four dollars. Sometimes, you'd hear someone in the audience yell "Take it!" after someone had reached the fabulous sum of thirty-two dollars—rather than risk it all for sixty-four. Or another audience member might call out, "You'll be sorry!"

This popular show spawned the expression, "That's the sixty-four-dollar question," referring to how you might extricate yourself from a difficult situation.

Less than ten years after my first exposure to this show, I was at City College of New York, hanging around the school newspaper one day in 1957 when one of the writers came in with a friend. The friend was Herb Stempel, at the time a City College celebrity. He was a postal worker/student who had won more than one hundred thousand dollars on the hottest quiz show on television, *Twenty-One.*

Stempel was an unimposing-looking fellow, and the fact that he worked for the post office and was defeating more sophisticated (apparently) opponents made the show work. Yet, he told me something odd, which I thought about only briefly: he was instructed to look as if he were struggling for answers even when he knew them. It made for a more dramatic show. I think Stempel wanted me, and others in the room, to know that he actually was even smarter than he appeared, that the answers were hardly a problem for him. I did not make the leap of thinking that the show itself was fixed, merely that it was altered slightly for effect.

But Stempel was to balk when the producers instructed him to lose to a more attractive contestant, Charles Van Doren (scion of a great literary family), and Stempel, who could not stop talking, eventually blew the whistle that the show was fixed—leading to the biggest scandal in the history of television or radio.

⚹

"I have a lady in the balcony, Doctor," was a phrase that used to make my mother, who liked to laugh at the absurd, laugh. It was from a quiz show called *Doctor I.Q.,* in which audience members were chosen to answer questions.

If the lady, or "gentleman," answered correctly, Dr. I.Q. would say brightly, "Give that lady ten silver dollars!" and the audience would applaud. But if the contestant hesitated, often someone in the crowd would shout out an answer, and the master of ceremonies—Dr. I.Q.—would sternly admonish, "No coaching from the audience, please!" This admonishment had an official ring to it, as if Dr. I.Q. might just haul the guilty interferer into a court of law.

Sometimes, when the people didn't know the answer, they were reluctant even to take a guess. I couldn't understand that. Why not say something, anything? Yet, the idea of a microphone so cowed some people, that they were, literally, speechless. When they blew it, they got a consolation prize: a box of Mars Bars, from the chocolate-maker whose most famous confections were Milky Way and Snickers.

But until beer and baseball were wed in the 1950s, no single product was so associated with the entertainment industry as breakfast foods were with radio. And nothing lured me like cereal.

Yet, ready-to-eat breakfast cereals were still fairly new when radio was coming of age. Quaker Oats first packaged cereal in the 1880s—until then, it had been in open bins, which meant there were extra added ingredients in oats, such as vermin, that people didn't necessarily want. By the late 1890s, Kellogg's and Post were packaging cereals designed to be eaten cold.

Still, there was a health-food aura to these cereals. Shredded Wheat, for example, was packaged as "good for invalids." Being regular was king. But breakfast cereals soon added sugar, and this created a new market: kids.

Even Wheaties had spent much of its advertising money on radio shows featuring a singing quartet. And then in 1930, it began to target youngsters. Meanwhile, a writer who had helped Skippy peanut butter in 1931 create the Skippy Secret Service Society came up with "Jack Armstrong—the All-American Boy." The sponsor was Wheaties, and the cereal became associated forever with derring-do and physical action.

Its first promotion asked kids to send in a nickel and a Wheaties box top for a Jack Armstrong stamp. It looked like a real U.S. postage stamp, which led the Federal Trade Commission to halt the deal—the FTC claimed children were under the impression they were getting a true postage stamp.

Wheaties also doled out fighter planes—American *and Japanese*—for box tops during World War II.

Two years later, the great cowboy star of the movies, Tom Mix, gave Ralston Purina the right to launch an eponymous radio show. Ralston quickly formed a Straight Shooters club, and you needed the Tom Mix decoder, or compass, or whistling badge to help solve crimes at home. The announcer created a badge imperative:

> But first, straight shooters, have you heard the exciting news . . . By special permission of your pal Mike Shaw, we will send you a whistling sheriff's badge. When you blow it, it will sound like this [whistle]. Oh, boy, can you imagine wearing a badge like this! Only a limited number of these badges are available . . . From the top of a Shredded Ralston box tear off the little circle with the letters "RSS" . . . mail it with 10 cents in coin to . . . Act tonight, tomorrow sure.

While Wheaties' signature "The Breakfast of Champions" forever was associated with Jack Armstrong, I believed that Kellogg's Pep had a more logical tie-in with *Superman*. The word "pep" of course suggested you'd be able to bound around, if not leap tall buildings. Kellogg's Pep was essentially the wheat version of its signature Corn Flakes.

Say this for Kellogg's: it went along with the great change in the show's theme when the war was over. Suddenly, *Superman* was all about fighting intolerance instead of the evil Axis. The home front was a battleground now. People of all faiths and races had fought together in Europe and the Pacific, and now it was time to bring that unity home.

One of the targets, incredibly, was the Ku Klux Klan. But Kellogg's, like most sponsors, was leery of offending any segment of its potential customers, even the lunatic fringe.

There was the noted Unity House episode, though, that evoked an admiring response from a wide-ranging array of social-interest groups, including the Boy Scouts. That emboldened *Superman* to go after the Klan—at least, a Klan-like group. For this it was applauded by the Anti-Defamation League of B'nai B'rith. The kids' serials—well, at least some of them—were facing real-life American situations.

Ovaltine, which to me tasted like the cardboard box the cereals came in, also reached out to children with its sponsorship of *Little Orphan Annie.* Then, as the audience for her waned, it shifted to the more modern *Captain Midnight,* throwing its resources behind the pilot and creating mugs and rings and secret decoder badges (no, despite what former children remember, Captain Midnight never had a decoder ring).

I never could figure out why anyone drank Ovaltine except to get a Captain Midnight secret decoder, or whatever other item the show was hawking. Ovaltine was sold as a healthful drink, but I don't remember what it was supposed to do for you. Years later, Ovaltine added chocolate flavor. Perhaps it is palatable now. Must be. It's still around.

Still, I went along with the drill and got my badge, after carefully removing the seal under the lid, writing my name "in block letters," and enclosing a dime in the envelope I sent out. This premium had not only a decoder wheel but also a tiny mirror in the center—to flash emergency signals in case I ever was stranded in a log cabin in the Rockies, or perhaps kept prisoner on some mountaintop. In fact, these very perils often befell the players on the radio, who invariably used their secret rings or badges or otherwise disguised signal-senders to contact those searching for them. It was a perfect fit—ads imitating art.

Ovaltine's romance with secret things had started in the 1930s with Annie, with its decoder badge for Annie's Secret Society, followed with one that had a secret compartment. After Ovaltine—a granular mix created in Switzerland—jettisoned the orphan for the airman, it produced a series of mugs. And then came the really interesting stuff: the decoders that brought us even deeper into the world of Captain Midnight.

During my buying years—the mid- to late 1940s—I heard of the Magni-Matic badge, which had a magnifying glass in its center. Of course, if you were out in the Yukon and needed to start a fire for warmth, you could concentrate the sun's rays onto a piece of paper, and—well, you know the rest.

This was followed by the Micro-Flash, with the small mirror. Plastic made its appearance soon with a Code-O-Graph that had a blue whistle in the center, and a dial for decoding on the side. Ultimately, one appeared that contained the tiniest of keys, to lock up something really secret inside.

And what mysterious facts did we unearth when I used my decoder? Yes, there were hints of the next show. But also, there were not-so-mysterious letters to decipher: "T...A...K...E...Y...O...U...R...M...O...M... T...O...T...H...E...S...T...O...R...E...T...O...B...U...Y... O...V...A...L...T...I...N...E."

I also had an assortment of rings—but had to wait until the war ended. No rings were produced from 1943 to 1945. Ah, but the wait was worth it, for Ovaltine came out with the Mystic Sun God ring. It was gold with a ruby—OK, red plastic—in the center. The stone, of course, was hollow so I could hide my most secret of messages.

I was tempted by the Mystery Dial Code-O-Graph, which unscrambled codes. I envied kids who had the Flight Commander Ring. There was a Whirlwind Whistling Ring, one size fits all. It was used most famously in the sewers of Hong Kong, where Chuck and Joyce were held prisoner. And even though I was too young to work in a war plant, I could have had an ID badge similar to those grown-ups who did. That was the Photomatic Code-O-Graph, on which you would insert your own picture.

The cost for these treasures usually was a pair of lids from the underside of the Ovaltine jar cap, and another 25 cents for "postage and handling."

Mail delivery in those months after World War II was haphazard, and magical. There had been "V-Mail," photocopied letters from my Uncle Arthur in Europe. They were read, censored, and then copied in such a way that they were downsized so the post office could coordinate more easily all those millions of letters being shipped from overseas.

From the day after I sent in my box tops, or jar lids, or wrapping (no bar codes back then), I waited for the twice-a-day delivery of mail from Leo, our gregarious postman. He whistled when he showed up at 8 a.m., just before I left for school, and also when he made his second delivery at 3:15 in the afternoon, just as I was arriving home. On Saturday, we got one delivery.

But my greatest treasure was that fabulous conflation of nineteenth-century sensibility and twentieth-century technology: the Lone Ranger's Atomic Bomb ring. It came out in 1947, when I was eleven years old. Trouble was, I had to eat Kix cereal to get one. Kix was a dry corn-based pellet, barely improved by smothering it with sugar and drowning it in milk.

I hounded Leo every day for this ring, though. When it finally came, I gingerly opened the package. This was, after all, radioactive stuff. I still remembered the photographs and films of Hiroshima and Nagasaki, and the rubble-strewn streets, that showed up in the newsreels after the bombs fell. The audiences in Brooklyn applauded. We were, after all, the good guys. I had grown up with the word "Jap" an acceptable epithet— even on children's radio serials, where one show was titled "The Jap in the Cave."

In order to see "atoms split to smithereens," as the ad for the ring had promised, I had to bring the ring into a darkened closet. The ring was shaped like an A-bomb. Once inside, I removed the tail and watched closely for the shower of light. I stared so hard at the ring, I must have produced rays coming out of my eyes. Perhaps I imagined that I saw the atoms split, perhaps not. I never took the ring out again. I had looked forward to this thing more than any premium I had ever sent away for, and it was . . . bogus? I'm not sure I thought of it that way, but I was terribly disappointed.

Quaker Puffed Wheat and Puffed Rice countered with a Royal Canadian Mountie in *Challenge of the Yukon* (subsequently renamed *Sergeant Preston of the Yukon*), whose signature closing line was actually spoken to his dog, "Well, King, looks like this case is closed." And Yukon King would respond with an "arf" or two.

Unlike most guys my age, I have never claimed to own a piece of the Yukon, which actually was a cereal promotion—a deed for an inch of land somewhere near Dawson. These real deeds were inserted into more than twenty million boxes of Quaker cereal and entitled you to that piece of land—if you could find it. And once there, well, I suppose you could put a dime on it, if not a house. If you like, you can buy one of those original certificates from a collector today for about ten dollars.

Although Sergeant Preston had a horse, Rex, what we all remember was the sergeant mushing with his dog sled, led by King, and Preston's command: "On, King—on you huskies!"

> Announcer: Now, as gunshots echo across the windswept, snow-covered regions of the wild Northwest, Quaker Puffed Wheat and Quaker Puffed Rice, the breakfast cereal shot from guns, presents *The Challenge of*

the Yukon! It's Yukon King, swiftest and strongest lead dog of the north-west, blazing the trail for Sergeant Preston of the Northwest Police in his relentless pursuit of lawbreakers.

Preston: On King! On you huskies!

Announcer: Gold—gold discovered in the Yukon! A stampede to the Klondike in the wild race for riches. Back to the days of the Gold Rush with Quaker Puffed Wheat and Quaker Puffed Rice bringing you the adventures of Sergeant Preston and his wonder dog, Yukon King—as they meet the challenge of the Yukon.

Music

Boy: Extree! Extree! Hear All About It!

Announcer: Yes, hear about how you fellows and girls can get a swell and complete model farm.

Girl: It's the Quaker Model Farm.

If there was a similarity between the Lone Ranger and the Green Hornet, there's a simple explanation: All three shows were created by the same people. But while the Ranger and the Hornet had trusty human sidekicks, Preston's was the ever-present dog.

Still, the Mountie went after the same type of criminal or criminals, only in a snow-filled frontier setting. The plots had gritty themes and evocative names: "Rebellion in the North," or "Last Mail from Last Chance."

And like the Lone Ranger ("William Tell Overture") and the Green Hornet ("Flight of the Bumblebee"), Preston also had a classical music theme (Von Reznicek's "Donna Diana Overture").

Chapter 11

Sports on the Airwaves!

My first baseball memory: It is 1946, I am ten years old, and I'm listening to the All-Star game sponsored by Gillette. Ted Williams is going 4-for-4—including two home runs. One of them is a meteorite shot on a Rip Sewell "eephus" pitch.

Four-for-four! Perfection. From that moment on, Williams was my idol. Everything he did, everything he was, fit into my belief system of life.

And when I learned that Williams himself was a child of divorce . . . well, the bond between us was strengthened forever. My uniform number was "9." My bat was a thin-handled Williams model. My glove had his neat signature.

That first game set the stage for me and sports. Radio took on a storybook, Frank Merriwell kind of veneer. With radio, and sports, all things were possible. I rarely went to games in the flesh; once in a while, my absent father showed up and would, unannounced, take me to Ebbets Field. But he was so argumentative with people, something always was bound to happen: the bus driver wouldn't let me on for free because I was more than six years old, or the ticket-seller tried to short-change my father, or a fan in front was too noisy, or the hot-dog seller wasn't polite.

But, as the guy sang in the Broadway show *Chorus Line,* recalling his travails growing up, "Everything was beautiful at the ballet." So it was for me listening to sports on the radio, where what those athletic heroes did put them in a pantheon for gods.

Little did I know that most of the baseball I listened to was a re-creation. Ersatz baseball.

In other words, the announcers really weren't at the game. Instead, they were in a studio, sitting at a desk with a Western Union ticker—which, now that I think about it, could be heard in the background—and which provided the bare-bones facts of the game. But the announcer made it seem as if he were actually at the game. Sometimes, the announcer also would be in communication with the press box by telephone.

He'd smack two sticks together to give the sound of a bat striking a ball, he'd turn up the sound of recorded crowd noise, he'd talk about a shortstop going to his right to backhand a ball, gobble it up, set, and throw to first—for the out! The crowd roared.

Except that Red Barber, the fellow I listened to on the Dodgers, never saw the play or even knew whether it had been good or bad, or how many balls or strikes were on the batter. Years later, Barber claimed he never misled the listener, that he always explained it was a re-creation. But others didn't have his integrity.

Classically, the announcer claimed, "Pee Wee is tapping the dirt out of his spikes, then gets set in the batter's box. Spahn peers down at him from the mound. And here's the first pitch: low, for a ball."

In reality, all Barber and any his colleagues really knew was the out-come of the at-bat as relayed on the yellow strip of ticker-tape. It would read something like this—"6-3." That means a grounder to short ("6," in scorer's shorthand) and a throw to first ("3").

The first time I realized there was something phony about this was a re-creation of a game I actually had attended. Sometimes, even at home games, the event was broadcast at night—but not from a tape done live at the game. It was re-created as well.

That afternoon, I had gone to Ebbets Field and sat in my usual sixty-cent bleacher seat in left-centerfield. The only play made directly in front of me was an easy fly ball hit to Duke Snider in centerfield. He took a step to his right, patted his glove, and made the routine catch. But that night, I happened to tune in just when that play was coming up. The announcer called it: "It's a fly to deep left-center, Snider after it—and makes a fine running catch!"

How could that be? I wondered. There was no running catch. I called the station, but of course got no one who could help me.

This re-created world, I was to learn, was part of the fabric of baseball. Most teams in the 1940s didn't have announcers at the games. And certainly there were no announcers at the minor-league games.

Sometimes, the announcer would do his play-by-play while sitting at a telephone, talking to someone at the ball park. Invariably, though, it was the Western Union man who sent along the info. But back in the studio, the announcer magically would come up with a host of interesting facts: clouds were darkening the field; or the first three pitches were high and inside, and now the batter was back on his heels, ready to tag a 3-0 pitch if he got the green light; or the manager was heckling the umpire from the dugout and was told to quiet down. And always, there was the batter knocking the dirt out of his spiked shoes.

Well into the 1930s, New York baseball had been the last holdout in broadcasting games over the radio. At first, the clubs believed that a radio broadcast would hurt attendance. Then, when it was apparent the thirteen other major-league clubs could still make a living even with radio, there was another, perhaps more valid, reason: because New York had three teams—the Yankees, Giants, and Dodgers—one of them always was home. If there were radio broadcasts of, say, two teams on the road, then home attendance seemed likely to suffer.

Thus, only opening games were aired. Sometimes, an important series also was on the radio, and there were the night-time re-creations. But in 1939, the Dodgers underwent a profound front-office change. They brought in the dynamic, unpredictable Larry MacPhail from Cincinnati to serve as the new general manager. The Dodgers were getting serious. They had not been in the World Series since shortly after the Great War, and had become a legendary laughingstock. Even their nickname connoted nuttiness: they became the Dodgers because, once upon a time, their outfielders played in a field without a fence, and when they chased the ball they had to elude the trolleys that plied the Brooklyn streets. From Trolley Dodgers they became, simply, Dodgers.

They were, however, my Dodgers. By the time I got to know them, in the mid- to late forties, they had become good, if failed, gods—always blowing it at the final moment. Wait 'til next year was their rallying cry. Like Sisyphus, they were doomed to start from the bottom each time they got near the top.

I grew up knowing this history: of guys with nicknames like "Frenchy," or of an outfielder who stopped a fly ball with his head, or of a flaky manager named Casey Stengel who once tipped his cap to an umpire—and a pigeon flew out. His predecessor, Wilbert Robinson, once attempted to catch an egg dropped from a building, using a catcher's mitt.

MacPhail brought with him the Cincinnati broadcaster, a folksy homespun gentleman named Red Barber. Forty years later, Barber told me how he had been hired by the Reds: He was told to report to spring training by their traveling secretary, a fellow he knew as "Scotty Rustum." Turns out that "Scotty Rustum"—the way the name sounded on the telephone—was James (Scotty) Reston. He eventually left baseball, became a working journalist, and wound up as a Pulitzer Prize–winning columnist and an icon of American journalism—for the *New York Times*.

As part of his make-over of New York baseball, MacPhail also brought in the irascible symbol of the St. Louis Cardinals Gashouse Gang—Leo Durocher—to be the Brooklyn manager. But it was the addition of Red Barber to the press box that forced the Yankees and Giants to leap into the electronic age by hiring their own full-time announcer.

He was Arch McDonald, and he was going to broadcast both the Yankees and Giants home games. His sidekick was a fellow who, according to legend, mispronounced "Ivory Soap" as "Ovary Soup," and soon was canned. He was replaced in midseason by Mel Allen—who was to become the most famous baseball announcer of them all. His signature call was "How about that?!" when a Yankee made a major play.

The next season Allen took over the Yankees, while Barber reigned as the Dodgers' announcer, bringing to Brooklyn his Southern-isms. So in New York, a pair of announcers from the South, Allen and Barber, became national figures broadcasting the quintessential New York teams.

There was an unusual aspect to Barber's broadcasts, which were sponsored in part by Old Gold cigarettes. If a Dodger hit a home run in Ebbets Field, he would be greeted at home plate by the bat boy—who handed him a carton of the cigarettes. For the moment the ball landed in the stands, or cleared the outfield fence, Barber would slide a carton of cigarettes down the foul screen behind home plate. Fans today might think of baseball and beer as being twinned—but back then, cigarettes were as much a part of the game. In fact, I still recall print ads featuring Ted Williams, Joe DiMaggio, and Stan Musial holding cigarettes, plugging the brand they supposedly smoked.

Those cartons of cigarettes sliding down the screen—what a bonus for the ballplayers! Imagine getting two dollars' worth of cigarettes for free. Interestingly, only one Dodger was ineligible for the cigarettes. His name was Tommy Brown, a wartime player. He was only seventeen years old when he put on a Dodgers' uniform (most of the healthy men in

America were in the service). But Brown was too young to smoke, and never got the cigarettes until he turned eighteen.

When the Yankees played the Red Sox, I often stayed home so I could listen to Williams's at-bats on the radio. By the time I became a reporter, he had retired. It wasn't until 1989 that I finally met him—and at Cooperstown at that, home of the Hall of Fame.

I had been there for the induction of Carl Yastrzemski, the Red Sox slugger with whom I was collaborating on an autobiography. And there, off by himself, standing under a plaque of Ty Cobb, the hitter he most admired, was Williams himself. I had always heard he was outsized, and he was. A booming voice, a belly. I circled him for a moment or two, trying to figure out what I could say to get a conversation going. The only other time I had felt like this—in awe of someone—was at a party hosted by Jacqueline Kennedy for a mutual friend, James Nicholas, the orthopedic surgeon for the Jets who had once operated on John Kennedy's back. I wanted to approach Mrs. Kennedy, but each time I did, I stopped. Finally, I said to my wife, "On the count of three, I'm going over to her." And I did, and when I told her my name, she said, "Oh, yes," as if she knew it. We had a nice chat about our mutual friend, while a few feet away, her financial mentor and companion in the final years of her life, Maurice Tempelsman, stood with a perpetual smile. She never introduced him, and he never joined the conversation. But she did tell me how our friend Dr. Nicholas "saved my husband's life." She was referring, of course, to Jack Kennedy.

Now, as I regarded Williams, I told my wife and youngest child, Mike, who was sixteen, "I'm going to talk to him. I just need the courage."

Finally, as I had done with Mrs. Kennedy—I told myself when I counted to "three" I would talk to him—I went over to Williams and thrust out my hand and told him our longtime columnist, Arthur Daley, had a special fondness for him.

I must have mentioned the only newspaperman in America that Williams liked, for he smiled and said, "Arthur always put things down accurately. He never made things up."

That got me started, at least. What could I tell him—that I knew his mother was somewhat of a weirdo, had been in the Salvation Army panhandling on street corners? That I knew he had grown up without a father? That I played hooky so I could listen to his at-bat—or that he was my earliest baseball memory?

You know, I don't remember what I said. I think we spoke about Cobb and batting. Maybe about journalism. It doesn't matter. I was talking to Ted Williams, I had met the man whose life had touched me in ways I could never explain to him. And he was smiling and talkative.

And yet, how many times in life do we get a chance to meet our heroes from the silver screen, or radio, or television—and what are we supposed to tell them? Would he have made me feel better if I had poured out forty years' worth of memories? Or told him how a ten-year-old felt? I wonder now. I wonder whether anyone ever had, and if so, how Williams reacted. Do any of our icons understand the role they've played in our lives?

When I walked away, on a high, Mike said to me, "You should have seen your face. You looked like a kid."

Chapter 12

My Feminine Side

"... [T]hat because a woman is thirty-five, or older, romance need not be over, that the romance of youth can be extended into middle-life—and even beyond."

Thus, my introduction to Helen Trent, who, in some fashion, I came to see as a radio surrogate for my mother.

Helen Trent was one of the ringleaders of the daily dose of shows that became known as soap operas. These aired from late morning until midafternoon—four hours of ongoing entangled relationships, family struggles, tense situations.

It has become fashionable to laugh at these shows from the distance—and safety—of time. But even to me, a child in public school, these ongoing dramas resonated with their monochrome studies of good and evil.

Although Helen was virtuous and loyal, her romances were always caving in, like my mother's. I could never understand why my mother never got involved with someone who would come over to the house, a man I could talk to. Perhaps one day she would even marry him. After all, these women on the radio were always meeting men—even though the road was rocky.

Helen's job even was similar to my mother's, who worked on women's hats in the days when a woman wouldn't even go to the movies without wearing one. Helen Trent was a Hollywood dress designer, and had a collection of famous friends.

Our Helen was constantly buffeted by scheming jealous women, or

even old boyfriends. Through it all, she had a relationship with Gil
Whitney, described by the announcer as "a brilliant and prominent
attorney."

> Sound: Theme up.
>
> Announcer: Lovely Helen Trent, deeply in love with the handsome
> lawyer Gil Whitney, faces the most desperate hour of her romance as Fay
> Greenville, an adventuress as beautiful as she is evil, has trapped Gil into
> a false promise to marry her, and is on the eve of announcing it. Yesterday,
> we heard Gil say to Helen . . .
>
> Gil: Darling, this was devised by an evil woman. I never asked Fay to
> marry me, but Fay is trying to force it. Somehow, I'll fight my way out . . .
> [Reneging on a promise of marriage was a criminal offense, and a staple
> plot-thickener once upon a time.]
>
> Helen: Gil, there's only one way—to find out Fay Greenville's past, if
> you could prove she's a notorious woman. If you could just . . .
>
> Gil: I've tried, Helen. Fay has covered her tracks too well.
>
> Helen: Then, Gil. I'm going to try. There must be someone, some-
> where . . .

One of the more fascinating aspects of *Helen Trent,* and all the other
shows that took up my days when I played hooky from school, was that
there were no Jewish names among the heroes, heroines, announcers, or
producers. Instead, they had rock-ribbed good old American names, and
for this Jewish boy, at least, came to symbolize who really were the
Americans.

The producers of *Helen Trent* were the ubiquitous Frank and Anne
Hummert, whose names I knew from other shows, *Just Plain Bill, Ma
Perkins,* and *Our Gal Sunday.* They also had a hand in, incredibly, *Jack
Armstrong, Mr. Keen, Tracer of Lost Persons, Mary Noble, Backstage Wife,*
and dozens of others.

The Hummerts were among a group of writers and producers whose
work was everywhere I dialed, on various stations, different days of the
week.

So Carlton E. Morse was the brains behind *One Man's Family* and *I
Love a Mystery,* which scared kids with shows such as "Temple of
Vampires" and "Murder Hollywood Style." Morse, born in Jennings,
Louisiana, met an assortment of characters during his college days in

Berkeley, California, and based his "Mystery" heroes on three of them. They were getting into scrapes and obviously escaped, for they returned a week later.

Meanwhile, on three of my must-listen-to shows, I heard the same name crop up. It was George W. Trendle, variously listed as a creator or producer. His *Lone Ranger, Green Hornet,* and *Challenge of the Yukon* snared me, and all had a few things in common—not the least of which was classical music themes. I discovered later on that Trendle wasn't merely a fan of the classics: the music was free. No royalties to pay Rossini for his "William Tell Overture," or Rimsky-Korsakov for "Flight of the Bumblebee," or Von Reznicek for the "Donna Diana Overture."

※

Our Gal Sunday had the famous introduction, asking, "Can this girl from a mining town in the West find happiness as the wife of a wealthy and titled Englishman?"

She was from Silver Creek; his name was Lord Henry Brinthorpe. Many of his lady friends looked down on her, but despite her quite different status, she was able to prevail with her not-so-fancy nobility.

> Once again, we present Our Gal Sunday, the story of an orphan girl named Sunday from the little mining town of Silver Creek, Colorado, who in young womanhood married England's richest, most handsome lord, Lord Henry Brinthorpe. The story that asks the question: Can this girl from the little mining town in the West find happiness as the wife of a wealthy and titled Englishman?

These simplistic introductions—Sunday, the "girl from the little mining town in the West," or Helen, "a woman over thirty-five," or "Mary Noble, Backstage Wife"—led to one of my favorite take-offs. The team of Bob and Ray, who somehow were able to generate funny shows five days a week in 1950s radio, came up with a daily segment called "Mary Backstayge, Noble Wife." They also spoofed *Mr. Keene, Tracer of Lost Persons* with "Mr. Trace—Keener than Most Persons." And don't forget their "Jack Headstrong—the All-American American."

Soap opera sponsors were everywhere: Ma Perkins's show in fact often was called "Oxydol's Own Ma Perkins." Other sponsors were Duz (*The Guiding Light*), Tide (*Pepper Young's Family*), Blue Cheer (*Backstage*

Wife), Ivory Soap (*The Road of Life*), Spic and Span (*The Right to Happiness*).

"And here's Oxydol's own Ma Perkins again," the show would begin.

> The true-life story of a woman whose life is the same, whose surroundings are the same, whose problems are the same as thousands of women in the world today. A woman who has spent all her life taking care of her home—washing and cooking and cleaning and raising her family. Before we hear from Ma today, though, I want to tell you about something else for a minute that will be of vital interest to every housewife listening, about a remarkable new laundry-soap discovery.

While I never did laundry until I got in the Army, those shows did help instill in me, and I'm sure Americans everywhere, a sense of basic values. The irony is that my mother knew nothing about these shows, and my grandmother had no time, nor inclination (she might also have had a language problem), to listen to them. Yet, I believed in the American-ness of them: the upstanding names, Perkins, Brown, Smith, Trent, Malone; the cities they lived in; the speech that was to be considered "standard American," as spoken by the announcers and the characters.

The soaps presented an image of American life, of family values, that I saw as a wonderful ideal. Imagine folks sitting around the living room, Pa reading his paper; Junior playing; Mom doing her knitting; the dog barking. The soap worlds were too perfect.

Anything I ever knew—or imagined—about farm women came from *Ma Perkins*. She was ensconced in Rushville Center, wherever that was, and the announcer called her "America's mother of the air." Her children were Evey and Fay. Evey's husband was Willie. Ma's business partner was named Shuffle.

> Well, today Ma's going to ask Evey and Willie a question she hates to ask. We know Ma's reluctant to interfere in other people's affairs. But for months now, we've all been wishing Ma would interfere about those cousins—put a stop to their wickedness.

Probably living in a nearby town was "Aunt Jenny," whose show was called *Aunt Jenny's Real-Life Stories*. Aunt Jenny lived in Littleton. But unlike Ma, Aunt Jenny wasn't actually in the shows. Rather, she opened the program teamed with an announcer, and they talked about cooking with Spry, a vegetable shortening. Then Ma Perkins introduced the show. When it ended, there was more talk about Spry.

The ubiquitous shortening was used in all sorts of food that, like the characters on the soaps, took on a mythic American aura—to me, at least. I grew up in a Jewish home in which my grandmother's old European cooking predominated. She kept a kosher home, and according to Orthodox dietary laws, dairy and meat never were mixed. You could have dairy with fish, and fish with meat, but nothing made from milk could be eaten within a few hours of having beef or chicken. Ah, but Spry—and Crisco—these were lard-free, milk-free, and could be used making cookies, which could be eaten with meat or dairy.

My grandmother spent a good part of the day preparing dinner, which often included pot roast, Wiener schnitzel, or chicken, including wings. But the Spry recipes I learned about included whole trussed chickens (how I wanted one with those tiny chef's hats on the drumsticks), and cakes slathered with icing. That's one thing she never made: homemade, icing-covered cakes.

We were never ahead of the curve when it came to food: no frozen orange juice because, well, we didn't even have a freezer compartment in our refrigerator. The Servel refrigerator was bought on the installment plan, and every month my grandmother sent four dollars to the Brooklyn Union Gas Company to pay it off. When margarine was introduced, my grandmother wouldn't allow us to use it on bread when we had meat or chicken—because the margarine, while vegetable, *tasted* and looked like butter. And butter, of course, was dairy. My grandmother wouldn't even buy margarine in a bag. Because the government didn't want it confused with butter, it would not allow the early margarine makers to color the stuff yellow. So the manufacturers sold yellow food coloring, which the housewife then added to the margarine in a mixing bowl. It was sticky, messy stuff. But then a meat-packing company came up with the "Delrich E-Z Color Pak Margarine," and another 1940s revolution—my, were we modern—was born.

"Now you don't need a mixing bowl to mix margarine, " said the announcer of *Nick Carter, Master Detective.* "You simply pinch the plastic pouch and mix it." For the margarine came in a bag complete with its little yellow coloring, but was white until you broke the inner seal and kneaded the whole thing inside the bag.

The first frozen product we ever bought when we got a refrigerator with a freezer—actually, all it had was a freezer tray big enough for ice cubes and something small—was a container of Birds Eye orange juice. That first morning, my grandmother took it out of the freezer and tried to thaw it. She couldn't do it. She attempted to break it up with a knife, but it wouldn't budge. Finally, she decided to put it in a pitcher of hot water. It began to dissolve, and, without thawing it fully, served the weak, slightly orange-colored potion. My grandmother did not buy frozen food again for years.

Yes, being Jewish meant making sacrifices, of carrying the burden of forbidden food.

But these people on the radio—they could eat anything! And such interesting foods were advertised: A Christmas ham! Pork roast. Rice Krispies Treats. Jell-O mixed with fruits (you could see the bits of banana suspended inside), or molded in the shapes of animals, cake mixes, brownies. And inevitably, there was an apple pie made with Spry or Crisco. Yes, that world inside the little radio box contained small-town America, with people who not only spoke proper English but also ate all-American foods.

They also sat down to the table as a family, which we didn't always do. My grandmother tried to wait for my mother to come home to set dinner, but some nights she worked overtime, or got on a subway train that was slowed because of rush-hour or work on the tracks or flooding, or whatever the problem of the day was.

On Friday nights, I left my *Captain Midnight* at dinnertime for the week's great meal: starting off with gefilte fish. (My grandmother would bring home pike and carp, whole, slice them apart, give me some innards to eat, raw, and then chop up everything with onions and spices, grate them together—invariably with her own blood that spurted into the bowl after knuckles were sliced by the grater—and came up with a ball of fish that she then boiled.) I'd eat it with horseradish sauce and fish eggs. Then there'd be chicken soup with noodles or matzo balls, followed by either roast chicken or pot roast. For dessert there was a compote of stewed prunes.

It was all soft—delicious and heavy—and as far as I remember, was unchanged from 1942 to 1958. I started going out on Friday nights about then.

What was the glamour of pork chops? I wondered. And how could anybody order a hamburger with a glass of milk! Yet, part of me was curious—why couldn't we? Once, I almost asked. It was the summertime, which meant I was at my grandmother's farm in upstate New York—the Catskills (or, the Jewish Alps, as comedians termed them). My grandmother had bought the farm in the 1920s, when her husband (my real grandfather) came down with tuberculosis. They lived on the farm for several years, with two daughters (one my mother) and son. And then, after my grandfather died, my grandmother moved back to Brooklyn and eventually married her brother-in-law. He, too, was widowed—after having been married to my grandmother's sister. It was common in the old country for a brother-in-law to marry a sister-in-law when their spouses died. My grandmother kept the farm, though, and all of us, from several families, would go up to this old place, with no electricity, no running water (there was a nearby outhouse), and no telephone. You couldn't even hear a portable radio because we were so deep in the mountains there was no signal. Every few days we'd pick up mail in town.

Much of the time we got our food from the locals. A couple of times a week we visited our closest neighbor, a farmer named Harrison Townsend (whose wife's name was Jenny!). He spoke with a twang and seemed, somehow, radio-like to me. He had blue eyes (no one else I knew did). He lived about half a mile away, up a hill so steep you couldn't get a car up it. This particular Sunday we were going to the Townsends' to get some milk and vegetables. It was about eight in the morning, so they were having breakfast. I heard something sizzling in the kitchen and smelled something I had never smelled before. Little did I know what it was.

"What is that?" I asked. "It smells delicious."

For the only time in my life, my grandmother hit me—a gentle open-palmed tap on the neck.

"Shh," she said. "It's bacon."

It was another part of the American dream I was missing out on—bacon and eggs on a Sunday morning. How the heck I survived not having this, I'll never know.

✳

But while my radio heroes never served traditional Jewish Friday night dinners—and certainly never had anything like a Passover *seder*—I could be part of the mainstream at breakfast:

Kellogg's Pep ("the super-delicious cereal"), and sponsor of *Superman*

Nabisco Shredded Wheat—*Straight Arrow*

Quaker Puffed Wheat and Puffed Rice ("shot from guns")—*Sergeant Preston*

Tip-Top Bread—*Tennessee Jed*

Grape Nuts Flakes, Cocoa Marsh chocolate syrup—*Hop Harrigan*

Ovaltine—*Captain Midnight*

Rice Sparkies—*Terry and the Pirates*

Wheaties—*Jack Armstrong*

Cheerios and Kix—*The Lone Ranger*

Ralston ("from Checkerboard Square")—*Tom Mix*

Cream of Wheat—*Let's Pretend*

Maltex—*Uncle Don*

Tootsie Rolls (for after breakfast only, of course)—*Dick Tracy*

Uncle Don also was sponsored by Chuckles soft candy. He had one of those voices that made you hungry. When he spoke, he sounded as if he was chewing, or had a mouthful of something scrumptious. Poor Uncle Don inadvertently gave rise to an ongoing myth, and indeed was parodied in *A Face in the Crowd*, and in Woody Allen's *Radio Days*. The story is always the same: a corrupt broadcaster, who has disdain for his audience, thinks the mike is off and says something like, "Well, that ought to hold the little bastards." And that actually was what I was told Uncle Don said about his huge preteen audience.

So it's not just today, in the Internet Age with its daily helping of rumor and simply made-up stories, that urban legends proliferate. For my mother related the Uncle Don story to me. I always accepted it as true. In fact, when I told my good friend Murray—a meticulously accurate fellow, who happens to be an accountant—that it was simply a myth, he replied, "It was true. I heard it."

Don Carney was "Uncle Don." His show began at 5 p.m., with a song containing words like "Hibbidy-gits," and "Sibonia skividy," and ending with "Sing Along with Your Uncle Don." Then he recited the Pledge of Allegiance—for which I stood in my bedroom—and every day I listened for his special treat: he would announce the name of a real-life little boy or girl who had been so good that a present was hidden behind the radio.

But his downfall—"that ought to hold the little bastards"—turns out had been attributed not only to Uncle Don but also to some guy in England in the 1920s, other radio hosts nicknamed "uncle," another personality on local radio in the Midwest, and even Bozo the Clown. The funny thing about this myth is that it was published in newspapers as early as 1930—yet Uncle Don remained on New York radio (WOR) until 1947. Clearly, he was not canned for saying this. For he never did.

Yet, years later, when a series of "Blooper" records was made, supposedly a recording of Uncle Don saying his infamous (and fictional) phrase was on the disc. Except that the average buyer of the record might not have been sophisticated enough to know that much of the "Blooper" series was a so-called "re-creation." The voices were not those of the original speakers. I remember one of them in which a sports announcer, caught up in the excitement of a touchdown run, blurts out, "Look at that son-of-a-bitch go!" It was a re-creation—of an event that probably never even happened.

I also am amazed at the number of people I know who remember Orson Welles's notorious "War of the Worlds" broadcast in 1938—when they were three or four years old. In any event, there was, in those old radio days, a gaggle of "uncles" and "aunts" and "big brothers" who hosted shows. It's an easy step from a myth about an "Uncle Wip" on radio station WIP in Philadelphia—reported years before the Uncle Don story—to another "uncle." Why, even a former station employee contends he was in the studio when Uncle Don uttered the words. And there is a report from a woman who claims she was in the studio audience in 1940 at New York's World's Fair when it happened (seven years before the studio employee was allegedly on the scene).

So it isn't just current nuttiness that infects much of the Internet chatter—you know, that people never walked on the moon, or that all Jews were warned in advance to stay away from the World Trade Center before 9/11. For years—centuries, probably—people have been repeating rumors of events they've never seen, swearing they heard it, or have it on unassailable authority that it happened. Thus, my wife's friend Judy tells us of a friend's daughter who's alone for the weekend with her fiancé. They get cuddly, and undressed, and, naked, he carries her on his shoulders and they decide to go into the basement to continue their revelry on the couch. As they descend the stairs, they hear a shout: It's her mother yelling, "Surprise!" It's an engagement party. Needless to say, everyone else is surprised, too, at the sight of the naked couple descending.

What I've never understood about the panic of some people listening to "The War of the Worlds" is that it was a production of a regular weekly radio show, "The Mercury Theatre on the Air." Listeners who tuned in, or who had read about it in the newspapers, knew that the title of that week's production, which took place the day before Halloween, was "The War of the Worlds."

Yet, the next day newspapers had a field day writing about panic-stricken listeners, some of whom wrapped wet towels around their face to protect themselves from the poison gas the Martians were using; or about others who ran amok in the streets, or those who holed up in the cellar.

But what this also demonstrated was the power of the word, the reality of radio—and that if you heard it on the radio—or now, read it on the Internet—why, it must be true. Even three disclaimers during the "War of the Worlds" broadcast that this was simply a drama failed to alert listeners.

As the *New York Times* noted in a front-page story the next morning, "Despite the fantastic nature of the reported 'occurrences,' the program, coming after the recent war scare in Europe and a period in which the radio frequently had interrupted regularly scheduled programs to report developments in the Czechoslovak situation, caused fright and panic throughout the area of the broadcast."

Thus, Dorothy Thompson, the prominent journalist and anti-Fascist of the time, writing about the broadcast in the *New York Herald Tribune* a few days later, commented, "Hitler managed to scare all of Europe to its knees a month ago, but he at least had an army and an air force to back up his shrieking words. But Mr. Welles scared thousands into demoralization with nothing at all."

Since most of those were adults who ran onto the streets, or jumped into their cars, or sought other ways to flee the invasion, imagine how real to children the daily radio shows were.

Over the years, in my job of writing for the *Times,* I thought I knew all the stories, the zany urban legends, the conspiracies, the plots that only someone's brother-in-law unearthed. You know, the one about the tall man walking into the elevator and commanding, "Sit!" Frightened, everyone in the elevator sat—only to see Wilt Chamberlain saunter in with his dog, which promptly sat down.

But something other-worldly happened to America after 9/11, and yet we've seen (and heard) it before. The attack created a mind-set of uncertainty in so many people, that there was now a terrorist-under-the-bed syndrome. How different was that from 1938's worries about Hitler invading other countries?

I noticed, post-9/11, that my e-mails were becoming . . . well, bizarre. Fantastic events were passed along to me as fact—as having happened to someone's close friend, or as having been discovered despite governmental attempts to hush up the terrible deed. At least, "War of the Worlds" was supposed to be understood as fiction. But consider the following, electronically shipped over the air as fact. It is all fantasy:

• The dreaded Klingerman Virus—which is brought to your door by the mailman in a plain manila envelope. Supposedly, you unloose a Pandora's box of wind-borne illnesses when you open it. Of course, the Klingerman Virus never existed. I suspect someone named Harry Klingerman from Boca Raton, Florida, originally sent it as a joke. (See, now I'm starting my own rumor.)

• The report, somberly presented as fact—even claiming it was once reported by CNN—that Israel actually once had Mohammed Atta in prison in the 1980s, but released him at the behest of our government. Then, supposedly, our government hushed it up by silencing the major news media. Israel even investigated this e-mail and found that a fellow named Atta (different first name) briefly had been held fifteen years earlier.

• How about this one, talking about a "scientist friend" who just realized that the United States's man-on-the-moon mission was a fraud? We never planted a flag on the moon, and man never walked there. And how does the scientist know this? Because in the photos, the flag appears to be waving—and the scientist informs us, there is no atmosphere on the moon. Of course, there isn't. That is why, before the flag was sent up with the astronauts, it was unfurled and made stiff so that it gives the appearance of waving.

• Did you hear about the terrorist and his girlfriend? He warned her to stay home on September 11—and then added, "Don't go to the malls on Halloween." I guess these terrorists just wanted to protect their women.

I liked it better when there were stories such as the woman in New York's Greenwich Village, who was carrying her dead dog in a suitcase—and a mugger came along and stole it. Yet, this was presented to me by a fellow sportswriter, my good buddy Mike Katz, as happening to someone he knew in his neighborhood.

But I must admit I've had my share of being suckered, too. I passed on the one about the woman who thought she could quick-dry her cat who had fallen in the tub. So the woman put the cat in the microwave oven and turned it on. The cat, of course, exploded.

Chapter 13

Fabulous Escapes

Announcer: Tired of everyday routine? Ever dream of a life of romantic adventure? We offer you . . . "Escape!"

Music

Announcer: Designed to free you from the four walls of today . . . for a half-hour of high adventure . . .

Thus began *Escape*. They were shows of literary quality: Fitzgerald's "The Diamond as Big as The Ritz," or Poe's "The Fall of the House of Usher." And the scary ones were every bit as frightening to me as sitting in a darkened movie theater five blocks from my house, watching *Frankenstein*, for twelve cents.

Indeed, radio's spoken words still resonate with their color and drama. You had to have good writing because it was about words and sound. Remember the campfire stories we heard as children? One person talking—and creating a universe of wonder, awe, and usually, to scare us, fear. I don't think my listening to the radio as a kid was very different from the way many societies still have a story teller, and learn about the world and their world from the spoken word.

Narrator: Lights Out, everybody

Sound: Gong—wind blows

Narrator: This is the witching hour

Sound: Dog howling in the wind

Narrator: It is the hour when dogs howl

Sound: Clock chimes, howling and barking dogs
Narrator: And evil is let loose on a sleeping world
Sound: Thunder
Announcer: Want to hear about it? Then turn out your lights
Sound: Noises diminish, gong
Announcer: The National Broadcasting Company brings you "Lights
Out" . . . Sit in the dark and listen to . . .
Narrator: Lights Out!
Sound: Gong, then silence

How I scared myself listening to *Light's Out.* But I had been warned: "Once again we caution you, these Light's Out stories are not for the timid soul and if you frighten easily, turn off your radio now."

Of course, I didn't. Thus, once a week for thirty minutes, from the time I was, oh, eight or nine until I was a teenager, I'd listen to *Suspense,* as well as *Light's Out* or *Escape. Suspense* was not science fiction, though, as many other of my shows were. Rather, I found myself listening to tightly dramatic situations that logically could have happened. These were, after all, as the announcer explained, "Tales calculated to keep you in . . . suspense!"

Sound: Clock chimes slowly
Announcer: Tonight, *Suspense* brings you a repeat performance of one
of the most controversial plays ever presented over your radio. It is called
"Zero Hour" by Ray Bradbury . . .
Music up. Scary version of "Twinkle, Twinkle Little Star" . . .

A wine named "Roma" was among the sponsors of *Suspense* during its long run. And if I thought that cigarette smoking was sophisticated, why, I was downright captivated by the idea of sipping wine, which conveyed a persona of sophistication a Cesar Romero would envy:

Announcer: *Suspense* is presented for your enjoyment by Roma Wines.
. . . Let's imagine ourselves in sun-drenched Havana, dining in the gay club
Montmartre. [Music] As you listen to the music, you put down your wine
glass to tell our host how much you enjoy his hospitality. Part of the credit
belongs to Cuba, he smilingly acknowledges, but part of the credit belongs
also to YOUR country, for producing this excellent wine which adds so

much to our enjoyment. For this is Roma Wine from California in your own U.S.A. . . .

The Man in Black [the narrator of the series]: And now . . . we again hope to keep you in . . . Suspense!"

There was a program about a mysterious hitchhiker who kept turning up during a man's cross-country drive; there was another about children playing with imaginary friends, who wind up joining her in a scary walk up creaky stairs as the show ends; the classic about a bedridden woman who, on crossed telephone lines, overhears people plotting to kill her. This was "Sorry, Wrong Number," with Agnes Moorehead, which became a film, and then was re-created again on radio. I once heard Cary Grant doing a *Suspense* broadcast.

I don't know whether it would have been easier listening to *Suspense* if I had a brother or sister to share it with. Deflect some of the fear factor, perhaps. But I was drawn into this clammy world of fear, as surely as I was attracted to those Saturday-afternoon horror films.

So I'd also lend an ear each Sunday night to *Inner Sanctum,* and the absolute scariest opening of any show: a crashing organ chord, followed by the sound of a doorknob turning, and then the creaking door . . . That door was opening to a supernatural world, where nothing good was happening. Yet, while it scared the heck out of me, it also had an insouciant narrator named "Raymond," who ghoulishly spoke tongue-in-cheek about the assorted horrors that were about to be aired. When the show drew to a close, there was that familiar creaking door, followed by Raymond's "Pleasant dreams," delivered sarcastically, if not sardonically. However, he also enjoyed a pun.

"Why, you're shivering," he told us in his weekly little talk with the audience. "Cold? Aw . . . well, don't let it bother you. Remember, many are cold, but few are frozen. . . . So, if you've got a little time to kill, let's do it now." The titles told it: "Murder Takes a Honeymoon," "Death of a Doll," "The Black Sea Gull."

That creaking door sound was so well known, it became trademarked, along with the famous NBC chime.

Inner Sanctum's sponsor was Colgate Tooth Powder, with a jingle that suggested:

Use Colgate Tooth Powder/Keep Smiling Just Right/Use it each morning /And use it at night . . . to help you rate with every date.

The announcer then explained, "Scientific tests prove that in seven out of ten cases, it instantly stops unpleasant breath."

The most mysterious commercial was for Carter's Little Liver Pills. They were a sponsor of *Escape*. The name "Little Liver Pills" itself was humorous, and the product—well, I'm not sure that even the people that bought it understood what it was for. My grandfather had a box of them. When I opened the box for the first time, I saw the little brown pills, which I thought somehow were related to liver. I was quite familiar with what chicken liver looked like, since every Friday my grandmother would chop up chicken liver with fried onions and rendered fat for our traditional Friday-night dinner. These pills were brown, like liver, and in my ten-year-old imagination, these pills did grand things for the liver. Perhaps they even were made out of liver.

But Carter's Little Liver Pills also became a national joke, and led to the expression, "He's got more (insert your own noun here—"money," "nerve") than Carter has pills." Essentially, Carter's was for constipation, and had nothing whatsoever to do with the liver. Eventually the government made the manufacturer remove the word "liver" from the name. Still, I remember:

Go to your nearest drugstore right now and ask for genuine Carter's Little Liver Pills. . . . The price, 25 cents.

Chapter 14

More Magic

The body and all its parts were scrutinized daily, if not hourly, by our radio commercials. Once the war ended, we could get on with the business of lubricating, oiling, cleaning, peeling, and scrubbing ourselves with everything that science could bring to a tube or a box. Colgate Tooth Powder was just one of many new ways I could present a shinier presence to the world, and Carter's Little Liver Pills was not the only medicine that helped you internally.

There was a host of bodily cleansers out there besides those little pills, with names that had exotic sounds and indecipherable meanings: Sal Hepatica, Serutan, Feen-A-Mint, Ex-Lax. Fred Allen's witty show was sponsored by the twin body enhancers: Ipana tooth paste ("for the smile of beauty") and Sal Hepatica ("for the smile of health"). Sal Hepatica was a mineral salt whose underground nickname was "the poor man's spa."

> Now, whenever you need that kind of medicine . . . it will cleanse your body of poisonous waste . . . the one laxative that combats acidity in your body

As if I didn't have enough problems figuring out my body when I was eleven years old, helped (or frightened) by my new microscope which showed me what saliva, or even the scariness of a hair follicle, looked like enlarged forty times. And my skin—magnified, it looked like elephant hide. Now, I had to endure listening to the mystery of waste management in my own body—acidity, poisonous stuff.

144

This weird science was perpetuated by the stomach remedies—no wonder a few generations of Americans came to believe that the body breaks down when you reach thirty-five. For that became a magic number when Serutan laxative became a major sponsor on shows such as Drew Pearson's *Things to Come*. For Serutan was "for people over thirty-five." That number also was the age that Helen Trent wrestled with during her daytime struggles ("that because a woman is thirty-five, romance need not be over"). Serutan contained "vegetable hydrogel," which sounded healthful enough. In fact, taking a laxative seemed a virtual necessity for someone of that age. Thus, it was "the different kind of laxative people over thirty-five are so very apt to need." Oh, really?

Besides being listless, though, you could be weak. And nothing was worse than a weak man. Listen:

> Announcer 1: Are they all talking about you?
> Announcer 2 (a woman): I know he never gets a raise. But it's his own fault. The company wants peppy, lively men. He's so pale, so nervous.
> Announcer 1: Well, mister, if you're listless, maybe you're not getting enough iron . . .
> Man: I was run down . . . couldn't enjoy my food. I now take Ironized Yeast and gain an average of two pounds a week. Thanks to Ironized Yeast, I now feel fit.

Just as Carter's Little Liver Pills evoked humor by comics who merely mentioned the words, or made a play on them, so did Serutan ("Nature's spelled backwards.") Nonsense jokes abounded about words that were spelled backwards and meant nothing.

Feen-a-Mint sponsored *Double or Nothing*, a Friday-night quiz show. Feen-a-Mint was a laxative gum—you chewed it, and got "gentle relief." Of course, the most famous chewable laxative was chocolated Ex-Lax. It sponsored *Strange as It Seems*.

Was there something in our character that created these maladies and bodily blips? Well, the makers of Bi So Dol mints, an antacid, had it figured out thusly:

> Today's fast, nerve-wracking pace creates hyper-acidity and causes the troubles known as "American Stomach." Bi So Dol helps neutralize the causes of the American Stomach. Only 25 cents.

Once our bodies were cleansed internally, that wasn't the end of it. There was dirt and smell to contend with, the most infamous of which was "B.O."—body odor. Thus, a magical bar of soap called Lifebuoy, tinted orange, just like a lifebuoy bobbing in open water, was the scourge of B.O.

> Girl: I wonder if I'll ever walk down the aisle.
> Announcer: Perhaps if you pay attention to this. [Sound of foghorn]
> Girl: That's the lifebuoy foghorn. You're telling me? . . .
> Announcer: Yes, everyone needs Lifebuoy in their daily bath . . . It stops B.O.
> Girl: I'm heading for a Lifebuoy bath right now.

Whenever an announcer said "B.O.," the letters came out sounding as if they were uttered through a foghorn. It was such a prominent, unpleasant sound, that the expression "B.O." worked its way into the language. As kids, we'd razz one another by claiming, "You've got 'B.O.'"

However, something came along that seemed to get at body odor where it began. There was Arrid, an underarm cream that would neutralize those negative scents. Hence, the following excerpt from the sponsor of a Hollywood gossip, Jimmie Fidler:

> Use Arrid, the new deodorant that saves friends and saves clothes. Used by Ethel Merman and other Hollywood stars . . .

One day, though, modern science figured out a way to get rid of B.O. without actually using soap. We started to hear about the wonders of chlorophyll, produced by plants but with the remarkable ability to absorb human bad smells. The major player in this newly discovered product was Ennds Chlorophyll Tablets.

> Well, friends, you'll be happy, too, when you see how quickly Ennds Chlorophyll Tablets ends Triple O—odor of body, odor of breath, odor offense.

Modernity always was problematic in my house—from electric toasters to frozen orange juice. But one day another new product came out that was sure to make life easier, for men.

My grandfather used to shave using an old-fashioned brush that he lathered up with soap and applied to his face. He used a straight razor, a menacing tool that required him to use a strop to keep it sharp. But in a nod to the twentieth century, he bought himself a Gillette "safety" razor, which was easy to put together, a small blade inserted into the contraption. Only the edge of the blade showed. It was impractical for cutting one's throat, say.

My more modern uncle, though, not only used the Gillette but also bought a tube of shaving cream. It was called "brushless," and was made by Palmolive. Imagine, you squeezed some onto your hand and then rubbed it onto your face—no soap, no brush, no lathering. The commercial promised a new world of freedom in the mornings:

> And now, here's news about the greatest shaving breakthrough in history. Palmolive means more comfortable, actually smoother shaves, for three men out of four. . . . Just get Palmolive Shave Cream . . . work it upward into beard, then shave. That's all.

But I imagined an even braver new world. So when I heard about a shave cream that came in a can—you pushed a button and out oozed the cream—I bought it for my uncle one Father's Day. Excited, hoping to make his life easier, I presented him with it. He examined it curiously, turning it over in his hands. And then he was going to try it! This was a modern moment up there with the arrival of our television set. He did not, however, read the directions, which called for shaking the can first. Instead, he depressed the top of the can . . . and some watery soap squirted out. He tried it again, to another stream of something that obviously wasn't shaving cream. But because this was a gift, and I was standing there, waiting proudly for him to use it, my uncle slapped the stuff onto his face. He took his razor and tried to shave. With his first stroke, he drew blood. That can of cream, unshaken, remained unused. Disappointed, I left the bathroom while my uncle looked for the iodine.

Then there was the mystery soap—Ivory. It floated. Why was this important? Well, since this was the era when we took baths, instead of showers, that little cake of soap would float to the bottom. Also, since women did laundry in soapy buckets, they'd have to squish around the bottom of the pail to find the soap. But Ivory was different. It floated! Not only floated, but it was, the ads told us, "99 44/100 percent pure." A few years later, when I got to high school, a science teacher explained that Ivory pumped air bubbles into the bar, which allowed it to float. As for its almost-perfect purity, it sounded impressive, and it connoted that it was better to use something that virtually was pure. As if, by using something else, there'd be impurities in the water or on your body. Turns out the 99.4 percent simply referred to the percentage it had of fatty acids and alkali, which all soaps must have to be called soap.

A statistic also was used to help sell another soap: Lux. For I learned in the commercial that "nine out of ten movie stars prefer Lux."

But soap, of course, also was for the laundry, which was done at home, almost exclusively. I remember when the war ended, the first Laundromat appeared in the neighborhood. It was filled with Bendix washing machines. Bendix was an aircraft manufacturer. During the war, all its resources went into airplanes. But not too long after we defeated the Japanese, Bendix began advertising these amazing machines that cleaned laundry, and extracted the water from them. Of course, we weren't getting one in our house. We were years from getting an electric toaster, after all. But about three blocks away, someone opened a store and put in half a dozen of these cylindrical washing machines.

Just about then, I began hearing about "the wash day miracle." It was called Tide, and sponsored *The Red Skelton Show*. "Tide gets clothes cleaner than any soap," the commercials claimed. Than any soap? Yes, Tide was not a soap, but something called a detergent. "Tide's In—Dirt's Out!" the commercial proclaimed.

The proliferation of soap ads was a natural outgrowth for that huge segment of America: a society whose moms stayed at home, and did the laundry themselves. So it was hardly surprising that the women who did the cleaning would also be the customers who bought the soaps, and so it didn't take an advertising genius to figure out that companies that sold what housewives bought should be the sponsors. But to attract listeners, the soap commercials had to be catchy and pithy, no long, extended explanations. So we all heard the clear-as-a-bell soprano voice of a young girl singing "Rinso White, Rinso White, Happy Little Washday Song!" She was "Bubbles" Silverman, who would be known in another ten years as Beverly Sills.

Another catchy ditty was "Duz Does Everything." Duz was perhaps the grandmother of the three-lettered washday miracle soaps. Eventually, there was Fab (as in fabulous) and Vel (as in marvelous). One commercial opened, "D-U-Z does everything." Then the announcer, Bud Collyer (who had taken off his Superman outfit), explained, "Duz clears dirt right out with no scrubbing, better than any other soap you can buy for wash day."

Ah, wash day. It was, I suspected, a mid-American rite. Imagine, these fabulous Gentiles actually only had to do their clothes once a week. My grandmother, meanwhile, scrubbed the stuff as it came in, morning and night. More reason to feel separated from all those people out there, the ones that used Duz and Rinso and Tide. My grandmother used a "kosher" soap (no animal by-products), a waxy thing that produced no discernible bubbles or foam and which required hard rubbing. After all, life wasn't supposed to be easy, was it?

✳

Use Halo if you want bright and beautiful hair. It contains no soap so it cannot leave a dulling soap film.

Huh? I had never seen a "film" of soapy residue on a person's hair, arms, legs, or anywhere else. Oh, yeah, I had noticed it on glassware. But now I had something else to worry about as I listened to *Mr. and Mrs. North,* the great sleuths. The sponsor was Halo, "the shampoo that glorifies your hair." Halo was a remarkable new product. It was a shampoo that contained no soap (hence, no "dulling soap film"). It had one of the catchiest jingles of the day: "Halo, everybody, Halo! Halo is the shampoo that glorifies your hair, so Halo everybody Halo."

As if film scum on my hair wasn't enough to worry about as I thought about the fifth-grade girls, suddenly I was confronted with another, equally demoralizing, possibility: that I might have yellow teeth. Not to worry, for as Pepsodent promised, "You'll wonder where the yellow went, when you brush your teeth with Pepsodent." It was the sponsor of Bob Hope's big Tuesday-night broadcast.

There was a parade of toothpastes that would prevent such ills as "bacterial mouth" (Kolynos) and "pink toothbrush" (Ipana, presumably preventing bleeding gums). Kolynos also promoted "that winning, successful smile that pays big dividends in financial and personal life." It sponsored *Mr. Keen, Tracer of Lost Persons,* and was described as a "high-polishing toothpaste," compared to a jeweler's polish that removed the tarnish from silver. It was an effective analogy.

While brushing my teeth was a value my mother instilled in me and the toothpaste companies reinforced, one day I heard a commercial for a dentifrice that practically ordered me to change the way I brushed— that it had been all wrong. The new product was called Teel. It was, believe it or not, a liquid "toothpaste." It was red, and came in a bottle. It had a slightly thick consistency, so it didn't simply pour all over the floor when I tipped it onto my toothbrush. And what was so good about Teel? The announcer on *The Life of Riley* explained:

> Only Teel protects your teeth from a certain type of cavity. You see, eight of ten adults have receding gums, and when gums recede, parts of your teeth are exposed that are twenty-five times softer than enamel. So chances are those softer parts are easily damaged by daily brushings with toothpaste that has harsh abrasives. . . . Only Teel has no abrasives . . .

Wildroot Cream Oil, white, in a glass bottle, was what I wanted for my hair to give it a greasy look. It was a sponsor of *The Adventures of Sam Spade,* a spinoff from the Bogart character in *The Maltese Falcon.* Wildroot had "soothing lanolin," whatever that was, and was "nonalcoholic." It made your hair slick, perfect for those of us training a pompadour. The jingle, "Use Wildroot Cream Oil, Charlie," was sung by a barbershop quartet which promised, at the end, "You will find you'll have a tough time, Charlie, keeping all those gals away."

But I never suffered from dreaded dandruff, which would have called for me to try Vaseline Hair Tonic, good for "dry scalp itch." Luckily, I didn't shave. Thus, no dreaded "five o'clock shadow," that growth of facial hair that began in the late afternoon. Gem razors would nip it in the bud.

The body, then, was this temple of garbage and trash.

Not to worry. I was bombarded also with remedies. When I listened to *Sherlock Holmes* and was suffering from a cold, I could take Bromo-Quinine. The pills came in a tin (sixteen for forty cents), and one of the ingredients was caffeine.

> Announcer: Let me tell you about a product that thousands of people now use to get relief from the pains of headache, neuralgia, and rheumatism.

That product was Anacin, sponsor of *Our Gal Sunday,* as well as *Just Plain Bill.* Neuralgia was one of those vague ills of the 1940s and earlier decades. Whatever it was, Anacin, with its famous "combination of ingredients," could stop it, along with the pain of rheumatism. It was, we were told, "like a doctor's prescription" because it contained not just one ingredient, which its competitors had. That pitifully inadequate one ingredient it referred to was aspirin. Another difficulty older people faced, I heard, was back problems. That could be solved by Doan's Pills.

Then again, there was the headache. What to do about it? The announcer on *Ellery Queen* gave us the answer: Bromo-Seltzer. It had the ability to "fight headache three ways." Of course, today's consumers might wonder why you would take an antacid to cure a headache. Bromo-Seltzer had both aspirin and an antacid. The reason, we were told, was that there were three components to a headache: jumpy nerves, upset stomach, and the pain itself. This led to what was called a "sick headache." Bad science? Of course. But when this child listened to the commercial, he learned about jumpy nerves and upset stomach and their role in causing a headache. Jumpy nerves, naturally, were a menace.

Perhaps the most famous stomach remedy was Tums—as in "Tums for the tummy." And just as a clever ad campaign had *The Fat Man* sponsored by Pepto-Bismol, with its implied cure for the over eater, the celebrity portly announcer for Jack Benny, Don Wilson, was the Tums spokesman: "This is Don Wilson. With Tums, you don't wait to fix sour stomach. . . . There's nothing to drink. Use Tums whenever your favorite foods, or overindulgence, or smoking too much causes distress." We all knew that Wilson was a fat guy, since that was the basis for many of Benny's jokes. And you got fat by eating too much. Wilson and Tums were a perfect fit, so to speak.

✳

One day there was great excitement in my house. My mother had brought home a box containing the latest postwar miracle: Toni Home Permanent. Those were the days when many women went to beauty parlors to have their hair curled and styled, a lengthy, smelly process that wasted time. But this company, Toni, came up with a way to do this at home. It sponsored one of my favorite shows, *Casey, Crime Photographer*, along with *This Is Nora Drake*. My mother went to the drugstore, and she and my grandmother were going to give it a try. Imagine, no harsh machinery, just some creams and curlers. It had already created a stir with magazine ads that asked, "Which Twin Has The Toni?" and showed a pair of twins—one with the Toni home permanent, another with her hair done in a much more expensive beauty parlor.

Announcer: Today you just can't tell which is the girl with the natural curl, and which is the girl with the Toni.

I remember my mother and grandmother clearing a place in the living room—our one bathroom was barely big enough for one person. They got out towels and creams and curlers, and my grandmother began to work on my mother's hair. They read and reread the directions from a sheet of paper. My mother sat there for two hours. The cream or whatever it was they were putting on one another had to set. And when it was done, and the floor was a mess, they both proclaimed the whole thing a mess and not worth the effort. Not for us was this modern stuff. Why, next thing you know, my grandmother would have brought in frozen orange juice.

But the most ubiquitous sponsors in the evenings, and the most glamorous, were the tobacco companies. Their ads virtually promoted the healthful aspects of smoking. They made inhaling seem as satisfying as breaking off a piece of a Hershey chocolate bar and letting it dissolve in your mouth. Thus, I smoked a Camel cigarette I had lifted out of a drawer in which my grandfather had hidden it.

The idea of smoking—it put me in the rarefied air of Hollywood, where on the screen actors and actresses routinely held cigarettes in their hands, and often drew on them during conversation. On radio, I discovered cigarette smoking's other qualities, which were certified by doctors. "... 113,597 doctors were asked, what cigarette do you smoke, doctor? The brand named most was Camel," I learned, listening to *Mystery in the Air*. Furthermore, "According to a nationwide survey, more doctors smoke Camel than any other cigarette."

How could they say this? It was quite disingenuous, I was to learn. For what the cigarette makers did was send out thousands of cigarettes to doctors across the United States. Obviously just a small percentage bothered to send unwanted cigarettes back. So Camel concluded that the overwhelming majority of doctors who kept those cigarettes kept them because they smoked them.

Camel came in a terrific package: the camel stood in front of palm trees and two pyramids, and the box proclaimed, "Genuine Taste—

Turkish and Domestic Blend" in front of the pyramid. The whole pack was exotic. It had a blue label across the top, obviously some sort of government stamp. And, of course, the contents were forbidden to me. Yet, my grandfather smoked them.

One day, I decided it was time for me to taste a cigarette—yes, in my mind, the idea of smoking was involved with a sense that it was not only good for me, but pleasurable. No one was home. I went to the secret drawer in my grandfather's dresser where I knew he kept his cache of pennies, nickels, and dimes—he used to count and recount them every day—and his cigarettes, along with a little plastic telescope that contained a picture of a naked woman. I reached for the pack of cigarettes. I tapped out one cigarette just as I had seen the grown-ups do. He had a book of matches inside that forbidden drawer, too. I had never lit a match. I put the cigarette in my mouth and was delighted with how easily it fit between my lips. But I was surprised and disappointed that, when I touched it with my tongue, it had an acrid taste.

Still, I went on. I tore a match out of the book and struck it. Nothing happened. I tried it again, and the sulfurous tip flared, burning my fingers. I dropped it on the floor, stamping it out with my feet, and leaving a black spot on the carpet. This smoking business was harder than I thought. I decided on another way to light the cigarette. I went over to our gas range, and turned on the flame. Then I stuck the tip of the cigarette into the flame. I withdrew the cigarette and puffed. Nothing happened. It wasn't lit. Then I recalled that when grown-ups lit a cigarette, they puffed on it at the same time. I put the cigarette in my mouth, and put my face near the flame. I drew in a breath—and was almost knocked back. It was one of the worst sensations I had ever experienced. A searing pain ripped my throat, and I felt I was choking in a soot-filled room. I opened my mouth wide and took in gulps of air. How long I walked around, dazed and frightened, I don't know. But I took the cigarette to the sink and doused it with water. It turned mushy and unappealing and so unlike the cigarette that Clark Gable took a drag on. I broke it up with my fingers over the garbage and buried it deep in the can so that no one could see it. Then I opened the windows in the kitchen, convinced the smell would make its way across the back yard to the neighbors, who would turn me in. I didn't touch another cigarette until I was a senior in high school, five years later. And then I tried filters.

But I still was living with this product that all of America seemed to be able to handle—everyone except me. On radio the announcer spoke of sending Camel cigarettes "to our servicemen in hospitals all across the United States."

Camel was America's largest-selling cigarette, but all of the cigarette brands were glamorous. All had a distinctive personality, a signature phrase. I associated my relatives with the cigarettes they smoked, as if my mother and aunts and uncles were defined by brand names, as if they were designer labels. My mother smoked Philip Morris, which sponsored Allen Funt's *Candid Microphone*—which morphed into *Candid Camera* on television—and Milton Berle's radio show. Philip Morris's distinctive radio voice was "Johnny," a midget dressed as a bellman, who would imitate a hotel bellman walking through the lobby looking for someone who had just received a telephone call. Johnny would announce, in a high voice, "Call for Philip Morris!"

Meanwhile, my Aunt Jean, the former dime-a-dance hostess married to my Uncle Sol, the bookmaker, smoked Old Gold. The package depicted some ancient gold coins, which I saw as fitting for both my aunt and uncle. The cigarette's catch-phrase was "Not a cough in a carload."

Remember—the men who know tobacco best smoke Luckies by 2 to 1.

That was the way Lucky Strike's announcer ended its commercials. It made a big deal of someone being an "independent smoker," which meant those smart enough to make up their own minds. This theme was part of Lucky's famous campaign using tobacco auctioneers, in their rapid-fire sing-song speech, supposedly calling out the bids on bundles of tobacco. Then they ended the gibberish with "LS/MFT—Lucky Strike means fine tobacco." I knew at the age of twelve what LS/MFT stood for, although I must admit I never smoked them. I didn't like the bland logo on the pack. Even seeing a magazine ad for Ted Williams, my idol for all-time, with a Lucky Strike in his mouth, next to the words "It's Toasted," didn't persuade me.

Luckies also had another advertising gimmick. "Reach for a Lucky instead of a sweet," it suggested. In other words, it turned on its head the usual suggestion for people who have trouble quitting cigarettes—suck on a hard candy instead. Now, Luckies was telling us to give up the candy for cigarettes.

Chapter 15

The Opposite Sex

This is what sex was like as my teens dawned:

I saw an ad in a comic book from the Johnson Smith company. It sold things like fake vomit, and "X-ray spectacles," and a microphone that would amplify noises from across the street—in other words, it was for kids like me to peek in on the neighbors. Then the company began selling a book for twenty-five cents called *How to Make Out.*

A few weeks later it arrived, a thin handbook with the following advice. If I were at a girl's house, I should have her sit at the end of the couch. Then I sidle up next to her. Because of where she's sitting, she can't move farther away. Then the book advised me to put my arm around her, this captive audience. Finally, I would take the bold step of burying my nose in her hair, and saying—and I remember this, verbatim—"Darling, your hair smells of jasmine tonight."

Ah, consider my role models in this new world: Archie, Henry Aldrich, Corliss Archer, Ozzie and Harriet, Junior Miss, A Date with Judy. To a lesser degree, there were the tough guys, too: Sam Spade, Johnny Dollar, Richard Diamond (Private Detective). Many of the commercials that attempted to make us better people—cleaner, fresher-smelling, while being a sophisticated smoker—also had a backdrop: sex. Well, not sex as we know it today, not a synonym for amorous adventures. The sex of my hot-flash teenage years was more about trying not to be stupid than about how to get to first base.

The shows I heard that featured preteens or teenagers rarely discussed dating—and certainly never kissing. Take *Meet Corliss Archer,* a teenager who had weekly difficulties—of a sweet nature—often involving her boyfriend, Dexter, or her parents. In one episode, she gets a job as a babysitter, but doesn't tell her parents. In another, she decides Dexter should be a lawyer, and attempts to pique his interest in the legal profession. Or Dexter sees Corliss with another boy, and mistakes the situation.

Corliss, after doing the opening commercial for Campbell's Soup, would then get involved in a situation such as this: Her father has a headache, and immediately wants to know where Corliss, his sixteen-year-old daughter, is, so she can't annoy him. "Probably behind a soda at Schroeder's," Corliss's mom replies. The soda fountain, the malt shop— it was where young America hung out. No malls, no pizza places. Corliss is soon home, though, and describing how she plans to win the local department store's "Sweetheart of the Year" photo contest. She asks Dexter to submit a photo showing her in a white strapless bathing suit. Not only her mother and father, but Dexter, too, objects. These were the kind of situations that Corliss created. I assume the rest of the country got caught up in these problems, not just me.

Meanwhile, *The Aldrich Family* began with a woman calling her son: "Henry! Henry Aldrich!" And he replied, in a squeaking voice that indicated it was changing—a sure sign of raging hormones—"Coming, Mother!" Henry was likable and unpredictable, with a sidekick named Homer. Comedy sidekicks or foils for the star invariably had goofy names, such as "Oogie," or "Dexter," or "Jughead." Henry's father was a somewhat wise person, not unlike Judge Hardy, Andy's father, in the old Mickey Rooney films.

It wasn't quite sexy, but *Ozzie and Harriet* did have a pair of young sons, Ricky and David, with whom I could relate not at all. Ozzie was a bandleader on the show, as he had been in real life, and was in one mess after another, until Harriet always figured out a way to extricate him. Still, these were the paradigms of Americana, Ozzie saying brightly, "Hi, Ricky," and Ricky responding, "Hi, Dad," and "Hi, David," to which David said, "Hi, Ricky." It was all pretty cute.

Although David was virtually my exact age, he didn't get involved with girls on the radio. I had to wait for him to get to TV to do that.

If there was one show for my generation that actually addressed girl-boy relationships—I am not using the word "sexual"—it was *Archie Andrews*. This teenager had a crush on the true-blue Betty, but haughty Veronica always was scheming for ways to steal him. Betty was the sort who stood by him during his weekly troubles, especially in school with the principal, Mr. Wetherbee. Jughead was the doofus friend, in impossibly entangling situations. If Archie had a nemesis, it was Hiram Lodge, the richest man in Riverdale and Veronica's father. Most of the "drama" involving Archie and Veronica came about because of her higher station in life. Rich girls, after all, acted and sounded different. The down-to-earth Betty Cooper was poor, but a regular gal. I don't believe Archie ever kissed either.

Night or Day, at Home or Away, always carry Tums

This signaled the start of Tuesday night's *A Date with Judy*—"the loveable teenage girl who's always close to our hearts."

Announcer: Dinner is over, the dishes are washed, dried and stacked, and the family settles easily in the living room . . .
Mother: Goodness sake, Judy, would you stop pacing up and down.
Judy: The most important school dance of the year is in two weeks . . . I have not yet heard from Oogie. . . . Why should he call me? There's so many other glamorous women.

Of course, Oogie calls—he didn't call sooner, because he didn't have the nickel—and Judy accepts his offer to go to the school dance. But then, suddenly, she is sad again. She has nothing to wear, she tells her parents. Believe it or not, it all works out. Believe it or not, I listened from beginning to end. Not once did they snuggle.

Similarly, Junior Miss had a boyfriend named Haskell. Their intimacy, like that of all the others of their ilk, was their shared guilty pleasure at the malt shop. Junior Miss's malt shop was in New York City, though, giving it a more sophisticated veneer. All those other shows existed in small-town America. No matter to me. They never even held hands.

Even the smart, smarmy detectives rarely went beyond the kiss. My favorites all took place in a *noir* setting, a dimly lit office, I'd imagine, where the hero was smoking a cigarette and had a cold cup of coffee sitting on his paper-strewn desk. Some had secretaries who never appeared on radio; the private eye would dictate to them. Others had wisecracking assistants, like Effie, who worked for Sam Spade. My radio detectives were clever, usually bored, and only occasionally forced to use their fists. No one ever put anything over on them.

Dick Powell had the world-weary voice of Richard Diamond, Private

Detective, whose talents included singing to his girlfriend, Helen, at the end of most shows. No sense in wasting Powell's singing talents. He called his girlfriend "baby," or "doll." Diamond is a former government operative turned New York City private eye. A typical show began this way, with Diamond being a wise guy about something before introducing the plot:

> Diamond: Hello, this is Diamond. Why can't people start their killings in December, when it's cool? Now, about a week ago I got mixed up in a case and before it was over I took so many salt tablets I was the best-seasoned detective in New York. It started last Tuesday morning about eleven o'clock in an apartment on the Upper East Side . . .

Typical, tough-detective, wisecracking talk. But it set a mood, as did the dialogue of Spade, whose jobs were "capers," and who always ended his report to the client, dictated to his loyal Effie, with his private-eye license number. It made the whole thing official. Spade, who was played by Howard Duff, went about his business in a good-natured, humorous way, his clients usually having some absurd reason to hire him:

> Spade: What can I do for you?
> LaVerne: My name is LaVerne. Larry—Lawrence—Laverne. I regard myself as a dentist-sculptor. I want you to get Mr. Julius's bridge for me.
> Duff: Bridge. As in teeth?
> LaVerne: Yes, he never paid me.

Another of my hero sleuths was named, believe it or not, "The Fat Man":

> Announcer: There he goes, into that drugstore. He's stepping on the scales. Weight: 239 pounds. Fortune: "Danger." Who is it? The Fat Man!

The sponsor was perfect for someone who obviously over-ate: Pepto-Bismol, great for upset stomachs.

Chapter 16

The Backlash

By 1949, when television was in its infancy and I was leaving my pre-teen years, the first stirrings of the anti-serial, anti-cereal factions in America rose up.

Radio and breakfast cereals had an often-acrimonious relationship with public-interest groups, nutritionists, and psychologists, despite the thrall in which the pair held children.

Sometimes, there were such blatant appeals to children that parents were outraged. Ovaltine had the chutzpah to ask its *Little Orphan Annie* audience to send not one, but two labels (along with a dime) for a special secret ring. "You may have some Ovaltine at home already," said the announcer, "but you better buy some more because you'll need some more anyway."

How cleverly the premiums were insinuated into the plot, as this was from "Annie's Surprise Party":

> All: Surprise! Happy birthday, Annie!
> Annie: Leaping Lizards! Golly! Jumpin' grasshoppers!
> Mrs. Silo: All together, children:
> (Sing "Happy Birthday")
> Annie: Leapin' Lizards! Are there presents, too?
> (Paper crumbling)
> Annie: Oh, look. Here's a box . . . O wow. Look, a ring. It's beautiful.
> All: Wow. I wish I had a ring like that.
> Mr. Silo: The rose stone in the center is the birthstone for October.

Annie: And that makes it my personal birthday ring. Daddy Warbucks
is a peach to get me such a swell present.

Then there was the postwar juvenile delinquency scare, fears of kids
running wild (see: *Reefer Madness*). There was, at the same time, a her-
alded investigation by Congress into the horror caused by comic books.

The *New York Times*'s noted radio (and then television) critic, Jack
Gould, wrote as early as 1947 that "Parent-teacher groups were concerned about crime shows and hair-raising serial thrillers" and their
"psychological dangers to impressionable youngsters and as possible
stimulants to juvenile delinquency."

I never thought listening to even scary radio had made me contem-
plate mischievous deeds, or promoted dark thoughts. Indeed, my radio
was about the good guy winning out, often because he was moral and
ethical, if not brave and strong. Comics, on the other hand, depicted
often ugly, glowering villains and women in suggestive poses and attire,
and generally painted a bleaker picture of adventure.

Into this mix came rock 'n' roll, generally credited to Alan Freed, the
iconic disc jockey working out of Cleveland. He took "race music" and
brought it to all us white teenagers. By 1957 in America, forty of the top
sixty "singles" were rock 'n' roll, led by Elvis Presley's "All Shook Up."
Writing about the music phenomenon, a critic in 1957 noted that at
these "concerts" attended by teenagers, girls wear "tight, revealing
sweaters . . . skin-tight toreador pants."

What happened to sweetness? As my junior high school days were
ending in 1950, "Mona Lisa" by Nat (King) Cole was America's song. Not
far behind was "Goodnight, Irene," sung by the Weavers, a folk group.
The first tentative dance steps I took with a prepubescent young lady
around the corner were to the Patti Page ditty, "Doggie in the Window"—
complete with a barking puppy. We danced to the show tunes from *Kiss
Me, Kate*. Or "Secret Love," Doris Day's big hit from *Calamity Jane*.

"Radio is an extremely powerful educational force," a writer of educational children's shows named Lydia Perera said in 1947, making the case
that all children's radio must have an educational component, "because
whether parents approve or not, most of the children in the country have
access to one of the approximately sixty million sets in the United States
today. . . . It is just too bad to let him absorb so much that is of no
positive value. . . . The prevalence of stories about crime and violence

constitute a shocking waste of time. . . . Multiply that hour or two by the millions of children of elementary school age; the total number of child hours wasted is appalling."

So there you have it—adventure for the sake of adventure be damned. Perera saw no good for children—for me—in just having fun, or fantasy, at the age of eleven. Of course, that was twinned with "crime and violence," which became a running theme of investigations into what we were listening to.

A year later, a parents and teachers group in Chicago organized a committee to help wipe out "vicious comic books and objectionable radio and movie programs." The head of the group described "the menace to our children" from "hair-raising radio programs."

The most influential media critic was the *Times*'s Gould. By 1950 he was writing, under a headline that said "Time For a Halt" and a subhead reading, "Radio and TV Carnage Defy All Reason": "If radio and television aren't careful, somebody's going to call the cops." Television had become important enough to be lumped with radio. Gould was distressed that the Saturday morning children's show *Let's Pretend* had just aired "Jack and the Beanstalk," but that the show was followed by a program about a wife being beaten to death with a beer bottle. Gould cited a statistic that during a typical radio week, violence was depicted on eighty-five programs.

Another study of seven New York stations found 3,421 recorded "acts and threats" of violence between 5 p.m. and 7 p.m. in one week. That was broken down to "15.2 such acts an hour." Funny, but I never counted these in my radio heyday. And I don't think my mother ever even considered this a problem, nor did anyone else's parents I knew. In poring over stories and articles and reminiscences to see the impact that radio shows and perceived violence had on children like me, I came across only one article about war and radio and what the broadcasting of war news did to youngsters. How ironic—that real-life killing and maiming and hysteria and horror, and its effect on children, got barely a mention. But see what a Columbia University researcher suggested back then: that listening to radio by a child is a "reaction as a symptom that there is something in the home that makes the child want to listen to *Superman* or *Gang Busters*." So we were all neurotic. Children of a certain bent would listen to *The Shadow,* and others would be inclined to *Let's Pretend*?

What intrigued me was that this piece on the war and children was virtually the only one I found that discussed what impact, if any, violence on radio had on children as I scanned articles and books of the early 1940s. It was only at the end of the decade, as television became a major player, that Congress and public-interest groups found problems with what we listened to on the air, and became inclined to see that as a cause of juvenile delinquency. In a way, I can understand it. Grown-ups didn't listen to my radio shows. Most kids had a radio in their room. But you couldn't help watching something on television—there was only one in the household, and it was a big piece of furniture in the living room.

Almost ten years later, with children's radio down to its last gasps but the new "menace" of television having captured the imagination of the young ones, a Senate committee, chaired by one-time Democratic presidential candidate Estes Kefauver, investigated the causes of juvenile delinquency. It looked at television programming and concluded, "Life is cheap. Death, suffering, sadism, brutality . . . judges, lawyers and law-enforcement officials are too often dishonest, incompetent and stupid."

The search for the old values caught the attention of Thomas Edison's son, Charles, who said in 1955 that his father had high hopes for radio's mass-education possibilities. Accordingly, the Thomas Alva Edison Foundation was created to present annual awards which would ensure that "our country's heroes and ideals should be presented in a manner that will capture the imagination of our boys and girls." It gave several awards, including one for the best radio program portraying America. Clearly, there was great concern that radio was corrupting children, not simply amusing or diverting them.

This is how stimulated kids had become: On Monday through Friday, during the after-school hours when they should be spending at least part of their time doing homework, there were six serials between 4:30 to 6 p.m. The Mutual Broadcasting System alone broadcast seven and a half hours a week of kids' shows, adding to the six and a half hours ABC spent on the air.

Worse, worried some child experts: the shows broadcast later in the day were lead-ins to adult-time fare, such as *The Fat Man*.

Dr. Fredric Wertham had studied new phases of psychiatry, which stressed the impact of environment. He also had corresponded with Freud. He had the credentials. In 1941 Wertham wrote a book about a New York City teenager who had murdered his mother some ten years earlier. Wertham detailed how the boy had been addicted to movies, radio, and the comics. Then in 1954, Wertham published a book that scared the hell out of parents. It was called *Seduction of the Innocent,* and detailed, often with incomplete or unproved statistics, the insidious effect comic books were having on children. He claimed, for example, that in the postwar years, only ten percent of comic books dealt with violence. By 1949, he said, the number had escalated to half—and by the time the book came out, he charged that most comic books had to do with violence. By extension, many observers believed radio and, to a lesser degree, television joined in this witting conspiracy to seduce the young. Come to think of it, I knew of no more violence when I was ten or eleven than what I heard when I was thirteen or fourteen. But I wasn't doing any scientific research.

"The stories instill a wish to be a superman," Wertham wrote, "the advertisements promise the means for becoming one." So? Not so many people were as cynical as I was when the book came out in my freshman year of college. "Trust, loyalty, confidence, solidarity, sympathy, compassion, charity are ridiculed," he claimed. Actually, I thought that radio—and even comics—for the most part did just the opposite.

"Nothing that occupies a child for several hours a day over a long period can be entirely without influence on [the child]," Wertham claimed, dismissing a contrary idea that "healthy, normal children" would not be affected.

In a congressional hearing on radio and television in 1952, an advocate for temperance claimed, "I can't keep the beer radio salesmen out of my house." But Congress also heard an industry spokesman cite FBI crime data that showed no difference over the previous five years between cities that had television stations and cities that didn't. Within two years, still another subcommittee was set up to determine what effect radio, television, and comics were having. One of its findings was that between 5 p.m. to 7 p.m. on weekdays, and from morning until 7 p.m. on weekends, children's shows were filled with violence, with a sort of frontier justice—a sock on the jaw, a quick-draw—substituting for duly established police forces. Why, those were the very same hours I spent during my impressionable years listening to the radio, listening to nonelected, self-styled do-gooders such as Superman and Captain Midnight and Tom Mix and the Shadow and Casey, Crime Photographer take care of all those bad guys. Often, they did it with a sock on the jaw, too. What had changed? Was it just a switch from the imagination to the visual, or was something else going on? Or perhaps nothing else was going on? In one week in January 1953, the committee was told of those "3,421 acts and threats of violence" that had occurred on the television.

Ultimately, the Senate recommended that citizens' groups form local "listening councils," and suggested that television stations monitor programs that could contribute to "juvenile delinquency." The subcommittee also suggested there was "reason to believe" that TV crime programs were more injurious to children than were radio programs.

A New York State Supreme Court justice wrote to the *Times* in 1958 that juvenile crime simply was a mirror of adult crime, that the $500-million-a-year pornographic industry was not started by young people. That same year, an article celebrating ten years since Howdy Doody hit the TV screens pointed out that the average child spent twenty hours a week in front of the television. I've got to admit, that was considerably more time than I had spent in front of the radio ten years earlier. Also, a Boston study pointed out—not without some sense—that a child reacts emotionally, not intellectually, to what he sees on television. I think I agree with that. Had I listened to twenty hours of radio, instead of ten to fifteen, I think the added impact wouldn't have turned into a negative. Imagination would not have been confused with reality, as anti-TV lobbyists claimed. Yet, even as early as 1947, one radio network was considering banning mystery and crime during early evening hours, an eventuality I'm glad never took place. What would I have done before dinner?

I thought it might be instructive, as well as fun, to get in touch with some of my contemporaries for their radio remembrances—and to see whether I could discern radio's impact on who they are, and what they were.

So I thought of sixty-something-year-olds whom I admired, and wondered what they would say when I asked them about radio. We know that Tom Brokaw and Colin Powell were doing their homework while they listened. I think we all did.

For many years, I wrote about the New York Jets' football team for the *Times*. I produced a book about the franchise as well. The most fascinating character I have ever come across, in sports or out, was Bill Parcells, who was the Jets' coach, as well as the team's boss of the football operations, starting in 1997. He took over a moribund franchise—something he has excelled in. Before that he led the Giants to a pair of Super Bowl victories, then resurrected the New England Patriots' operation, bringing them as a far as a Super Bowl. He turned four teams from losers to winners, and went on to generate a 10-6 Cowboys' record in his first season in Dallas after that franchise had fallen on hard times and consistently produced 5-11 teams.

Parcells's style is psychological as well as physical, and always intimidating. He once stood over a place-kicker, casting a shadow on the football as the kicker approached the ball. "He was just messing with my head, see if I would flinch," said the kicker.

I remember on Parcells's second day of training camp with the Jets, a team he inherited after it produced a franchise-low 1-15 record. He stopped practice suddenly, then gathered around him all his assistant coaches—and proceeded to curse and criticize them for five minutes, while the players stood by, open-mouthed. It was for effect, sure, but it was obvious it wasn't going to be business as usual around the Jets. He had no patience for injured players, once referring to a Patriots' wide receiver who didn't practice as "she."

And what did this tough-minded, take-no-prisoners future Hall of Fame coach tell me was his favorite radio show?

"*Baby Snooks,*" he said, citing the Fanny Brice comedy show.

But he also enjoyed *The Green Hornet,* the man of mystery who caught bad guys, and, perhaps, more telling to me, *Tennessee Jed.* I was fascinated with what part of that cowboy radio show Parcells recalled.

"I remember the beginning," said Parcells. It started with Jed's sidekick shouting, "There he goes, Tennessee. Get him. Bang! Got him dead center!"

Now, that's more like Parcells. Right between the eyes.

His other favorite shows he listened to on his Bendix radio were *The Shadow,* and what he recalled was "a kid's show with Uncle Don." Asked how they fueled his imagination, Parcells replied, "I was scared to death listening to *Inner Sanctum.*" Hard to believe, but he had the same fears as the rest of us.

Parcells likes to tell the story of how he had got beaten up "bad" when he was five years old. "You gotta go back out there," his father told him. That could explain *Tennessee Jed,* and *The Shadow.*

But *Baby Snooks*? I rarely listened to that show, which was on once a week and featured Brice, the former Ziegfeld Follies star (portrayed famously by Barbra Streisand in *Funny Girl*). *Snooks* was sponsored by

Jell-O, and was essentially a series of gags uttered by the mischievous child of an uncertain age. Take this one, in which her father, Lancelot (she also had a brother, Robespierre), was trying to take a nap before being examined by a doctor for a life insurance company:

> Daddy: Now can't you go away and let me sleep? The doctor will be here in an hour. Perhaps you don't understand how important this is.
> Snooks: Perhaps I don't.
> Daddy: If something happens to me, you'll get a lot of money.
> Snooks: How much?
> Daddy: Oh, maybe ten thousand dollars.
> Snooks: Daddy?
> Daddy: What?
> Snooks: Can I have a dime in advance? I'll give it back to you.
> Daddy: When?
> Snooks: When I get the ten thousand dollars.

Thinking about it, perhaps there was something in Snooks's wise-ass responses that Parcells liked. After all, the child is father to the man, as the poet wrote in pre-NFL days.

"Children must have this kind of vicarious adventure," said a mother of two in 1947. She also happened to be an adviser to the *Superman* and *Hop Harrigan* radio shows, but what she said hardly was mere self-serving. "Normal children not only can 'take it,'" she said, "but need it." She was right. I got "intense pleasure" out of radio, which she claimed was a good thing.

※

Television kicked kids' radio off the air and created an expanded universe of programming radio never imagined. But not, I contend, an expansion of the mind.

But the serials and cereals of radio also played a role in their own demise, although it took a few years. For at the very moment in time when TV burst upon the American consciousness, and cereals deserted radio, pouring advertising money into television instead, the cereal-makers decided to spike their food with sugar. Once upon a time, there was something called "Shredded Ralston" ("Gives you lots of cowboy energy"). Youngsters had no choice but to eat such bland food. A nutritionist recommended, though, that parents not bribe their babies by sweetening the oatmeal, and even suggested that sugar be kept off the table when older children are eating. Even Raisin Bran, invented in 1942, had less than 11 percent sugar. But by 1950, Frosted Flakes was infused with 29 percent sugar. In 1953, Sugar Smacks weighed in with, believe it or not, 53 percent sugar. General Mills struck back at Kellogg's with Trix and Cocoa Puffs and Lucky Charms, all right at 50 percent. Now cereals had become not food, but dessert, sugared and crinkly coated, turning youngsters, many feared, into wide-eyed attention-deficit disorder cases before the term even was invented.

I was in high school in the early fifties, and got a part-time job for a marketing firm testing colored and sugared cereals for children. In one experiment, I was asked to give out three boxes of the identical cereal, except each flake was colored differently. Then I asked neighborhood children to try all three. Each preferred the taste of one color over another—the power of suggestion. Within a year, I saw these colorful cereals hit the market. The color, and not the content, was the reason the cereals sold.

That was just about the time that Kellogg's brought out Sugar Frosted Flakes and its 29 percent sugar content. Two years later, General Mills brought in Trix, elevating the sugar content virtually to half. Also, the cereals came in a rainbow variety of colors, many of them artificially produced. They caused headaches, said some parents; they created allergies; they were not the simple, natural food of just a few years earlier.

The cereals, which were now considered problematic, were the sponsors of suddenly problematic kids' radio shows, my radio shows. Well, if not completely mine by then, still a very recent memory. General Mills wound up sponsoring more shows on television, where it promptly put its money in the mid-1950s, than it ever did on radio.

Indeed, by 1958, Ralston-Purina's advertising agency bragged that it had stopped putting premiums in Ralston and Wheat Chex and Rice Chex—let alone asking kids to send away the box tops. It put its advertising money into prime-time (evening) television, appealing to the whole family and not just children. "Look, Ma, No Premiums!" shouted one ad. Clearly, there was no money going into kids' radio by then.

In 1955, the *Times* described the debut on television of *The Mickey Mouse Club* as "bordering on the disastrous," and cited the glut of cereal commercials as being part of the problem. That same year, Quaker Oats put a free movie ticket into eighty million boxes of cereals as part of a promotion with MGM, which was attempting to lure children away from television and back to movies. Alas for radio, it could offer no such promotions.

Wheaties also gave ammunition to the TV watchdogs looking for insidious hidden persuaders. If Wheaties made one calculated misstep, it probably was the way it handled its sponsorship of *Ding Dong School,* one of the early television shows directed at young children. For the teacher, Frances Horwich, incorporated Wheaties into her otherwise low-keyed schoolroom that featured hand puppets and singing. She placed a bowl of Wheaties on the table and said, "Now, boys and girls— when it's breakfast time or lunchtime or suppertime, what are you going to do? You're going to fill the bowl with Wheaties. Say it . . . Wheaties. The Breakfast of Champions!"

Eventually, Wheaties took sideways steps, morphing into Total, and Corn Flakes into Special K, as governmental and public-interest groups forced the cereal manufacturers to make cereals healthful.

By then, it was too late for radio.

My paper, the *New York Times,* had this short item in its daily "Radio and TV News" on April 3, 1949:

> The adventures of *The Lone Ranger,* idol of the small fry radio listeners, will come to the television screen in a series of half-hour film presentations to be made in Hollywood. General Mills . . . is said to have earmarked about $1 million to make a fifty-two week series . . .

And yet, when *The Lone Ranger* finally did arrive on television, sponsored by the cereal company, one critic was disappointed—the shows had cliff-hanger endings. It forced the kids to wait until the next show, just as radio did.

"Television has a better record than radio in the matter of children's programs," the critic noted, "chiefly because it largely has sidestepped the temptation to put commercial selfishness before the best interests of young viewers."

Funny, but I never thought I was being manipulated by "commercial selfishness" on my radio shows just because I had to "tune in next time." And I also never thought that any television show for youngsters was better than the programs I listened to—especially the ones that made the jump from radio to TV, such as *The Lone Ranger,* or *Superman.* Indeed, I always believed the TV versions were cheesier, and hardly any different at all from the "chapters" (our word for the serials) I watched in my local movie theater every Saturday afternoon.

Remember my earlier reflection on radio: I looked back at a newspaper for a typical day in 1948, when I was eleven years old, and saw my evening begin with *Dick Tracy,* and go on to *Superman* and *Terry and the Pirates* and *Captain Midnight* and *Jack Armstrong* and *Tom Mix.* Then, finally, *The Lone Ranger.*

In putting that era in perspective, to see what I had lost, I jumped ahead five years in my research to a 1953 newspaper, and looked over the radio listings to see what was on. Only *The Lone Ranger* remained on radio, same time, same station. What was on instead of the other shows I had listened to? They had been replaced by *Songs of the Bar-B-Bar* and *Bobby Sherwood* and *Twilight Songs.* Where had all my heroes gone? Where, I wonder now, had my childhood gone? Were these shows only an illusion, a moment that seems larger because it is so far away?

Instead, most of the children's shows were swept away. Those that made it to TV languished. Others were created solely for television, and many of these were transferred to Saturday morning programming. What the effect of these morning shows had was to keep kids at home when it was sunny outside—it wasn't a reward for a full day of school and play, as were my evening radio shows. Instead, these television shows started the children's day, kept them in the house, hardly thinking, eyes glued to a television just at the time of day when they should be exploring, or talking to friends, or playing. The line-up of deadening shows included:

9:30-10: Children's Theater
10:00: Western film
10:15: Lash of the West
10:30: Juvenile Jury
10:30: Rootie Kazootie
11:00: Saturday Stagecoach
11:00: Happy's Party
11:00 Space Patrol
11:30: Smilin' Ed's Gang
11:30: Kids and Company

By the time I had thrown away childish things, I had little interest in watching so-called kids' shows on television. Actually, the only one I remember even taking a glance at—besides the disappointing *Superman* and a derivative *Lone Ranger* that was no more than a shortened, second-rate "B" movie—was *Captain Video*. It is memorable for its kitschiness. Its outfits came from a second-hand costume store. Captain Video actually was supposed to be an electronics whiz who used modern gadgets such as his opticon scillometer to combat Hing Foo Sung, "the wily Oriental," and the sinister scientist, Dr. Pauli. Much of the show took place in Captain Video's lab, which had a myriad of flashing lightbulbs. It was hard to tell when things went wrong during the no-frills broadcast before the era of tape, because the whole show seemed like one mistake. It lured kids in with a cereal introduction, accompanied by a Morse Code ticker: "P-O-S-T . . . P-O-S-T . . . the cereals you like the most. The cereals made by Post take you to the secret mountain retreat of Captain Video!"

Perhaps I was already too old, having just turned thirteen, when we got our television set. Perhaps if I were a preteen I might have appreciated *Ding Dong School* in the morning, presided over by a portly lady with her hair tied back in a bun—Miss Frances—who looked like every schoolteacher I ever had, and who in addition to hawking Wheaties waved and rang a bell to signal the start of class. And then in the afternoons there was *Kukla, Fran and Ollie,* a pair of hand puppets with a live lady. No Fury Shark there.

Chapter 17

Different Time, Different Station

I took a dangerous turn as I came to the end of writing this book. I decided to listen again to my radio shows, to see if they stood the test of time. Even more, to try to discover what part of me remained with them, and why they remained with me. I discovered the Internet could generate sound bites and written dialogue of the old shows.

Among them was *Dragnet*. I had listened to its debut on the radio in 1949, and was smitten with its documentary style. I never had heard anything like it before—a cop talking low-key, matter-of-factly, with dialogue moving everything along. No wise-guy patter. No one getting hit over the head, and I never heard a shot fired.

Announcer: Ladies and gentlemen: The story you are about to hear is true. The names have been changed to protect the innocent.

That classic beginning—as I listen to it now, I'm still grabbed. It played to the audience's intelligence. No frills. Serious.

Announcer: You're a detective-sergeant. You're assigned to robbery detail. You get a call that a downtown hotel has been held up by a bandit who carries a sawed-off shotgun. Your job—find him.
Joe Friday: It was Sunday, October 9. It was cool in Los Angeles. We were working the night watch out of Robbery Detail. My partner's Frank Smith. My name's Friday . . .

But most of the shows I listened to had nothing to do with real-life crime dramas. Would *Jack Armstrong* sound goofy to my ears some 50 years later?

> Announcer: So Billy and Betty are driving out alone to Uncle Jim's office at the airplane factory with an important-looking letter that they've just picked up at the post office. Listen . . .
>
> Billy: Say, Betty, this looks like an important letter for Uncle Jim. Sure hope he's at the airport factory.
>
> Betty: Well, it ought to be important, Billy, with all those stamps on it!
>
> Billy: I'll say. Came all the way from the Philippines in a clipper ship. Gosh, wouldn't I like to make that trip.
>
> Betty: Well, I hope that doesn't mean that Uncle Jim will have to go to the Philippines.
>
> Billy: I hope it does, Betty. Then maybe we can go with him.
>
> Betty: There's the factory. But, Billy—the shades to Uncle Jim's office are pulled down.

Hmm. Could I doubt, even now, that something exciting (and dangerous) was afoot? And how about that letter being sent by a "clipper ship"? And how important it must have been because it had "all those stamps on it." Imagine a world that was conjured up just because a letter had a string of stamps across the top. But I knew what Betty meant.

And *Captain Midnight?* Well, I think I knew he always was corny. After all, his nemesis was named Ivan Shark. And how many decent parents have a daughter named Fury? But remember, we're talking 1940s-style corny, when bad guys really were bad and we didn't examine the psyches of outlaws and other criminals.

> Announcer: No sooner had Captain Midnight made a safe landing, however, than the ground proved to be nothing more than a thin crust through which the landing wheels quickly settled into the muck beneath, trapping the plane. Listen as Chuck cries . . .
>
> Chuck: The wheels are down to the hubs, Red. Oh, now we'll never fly this ship out of here.
>
> Señor Perada (whom Midnight came to save): It is indeed the unfortunate situation. It is I who have caused it. . . . My evil star will lead you to no good.

Captain Midnight: Oh, come, Señor. Your terrible experiences have deprived you of all hope.

Perada: You have said the very true words, El Cap-i-tan. There is no hope for me. . . . My daughter is gone. My cattle and lands have been taken away. Leave me, Señors, before you lose your lives in attempts to save mine.

Captain Midnight: Such a course would be unthinkable, Señor. Chuck and I are here to help you and we'll do so even if . . . but let's eliminate every consideration of such a nature. We can't lose unless we lose faith in ourselves and in our cause.

Perada: Ah, Señor. The words that come from your lips give me new courage. I will fight this man who has almost destroyed me.

Captain Midnight: That's the stuff, Señor Perada. We'll lick Ivan Shark yet.

Perada: Ivan Shark did you say? Who is he?

Captain Midnight: I will explain, Señor. The man who calls himself Douglas Chadwick is an international criminal. His name is really Ivan Shark.

I note now the formal speech of the Spaniard. It is a typical radio device of that era, showing the good guy. Then again, some of Hemingway's characters are no less formal in translation. So Perada's "evil star" is at work, and the señor gallantly tells Midnight to leave and save himself. Midnight, of course, would have none of it.

Then I tuned in to Archie, who, it turned out, hadn't done his Christmas shopping yet. Nor had Jughead, nor Betty, nor Veronica—nor even Mr. Andrews, Archie's dad. It turned out they all wound up at the department store at the same time, shopping for gifts for one another. A typical show, except that usually Veronica was trying to outdo Betty for Archie's affections.

Meanwhile, Sergeant Preston of the Mounties was trying to sort out the truth—was the sled driver for the mining company lying when he said that someone had hit him on the head and stolen twenty-five thousand dollars in gold dust, or was he in cahoots with the alleged bandit? Actually, he was set up by Pierre, an abominable French fur trapper who spoke with an evil accent.

Far to the south of the Northwest Territories, the Lone Ranger had his own problems:

Announcer: In the sandy vastness of Arizona Territory, there was no town more cheerless and foreboding than Quartzville. Situated in the midst of arid, dun-colored hills, it sprawled like a tired dog in the never-ending sun. Yet, it was beneath these grim, volcanic hills that Nature had stored her richest silver ore. . . . it was in the deep shaft of one of them that disaster struck without warning late one afternoon. . . . A tremendous explosion hurled tons of rock and gravel . . . over twenty men were sealed in a tomb, condemned to living death.

I thought that was pretty good, for the 1940s or even for sixty years later. And all the while, the background strains of "The William Tell Overture" were giving a moody, portentous sense to the whole thing. The story got even more heated when an itinerant, hammy Shakespearean actor (you know, the kind that used to inhabit the Old West), down on his luck and with a hole in his shoe, picked up a piece of paper from a bar-room table and stuffed it in his shoe. Of course, that paper contained a treasure map. I'd listen to that show any day to see how it came out.

I have made a remarkable discovery in revisiting my shows. We know, of course, that the Lone Ranger was the great-uncle of the Green Hornet. But what I have just come to realize is that the producer of both, George W. Trendle, also stole from himself in the introduction to each show. It was as if he had cut and pasted his own dialogue from one to the other.

Green Hornet Narrator: With his faithful Filipino valet, Kato, Britt Reid, daring young publisher, matches wits with racketeers and saboteurs . . . risking his life that criminals and enemy spies will feel the weight of the law by the sting of the Green Hornet . . . the Green Hornet strikes again!

Now for the great-uncle:

Lone Ranger Narrator: With his faithful Indian companion, Tonto, the daring and resourceful masked rider of the Plains led the fight for law and order in the early Western United States. Nowhere in the pages of history can one find a greater champion of justice. Return with us now to those thrilling days of yesteryear . . . from out of the past come the thundering hoofbeats of the great horse, Silver. The Lone Ranger rides again!

Both had "faithful" sidekicks; both were "daring"; one "strikes again," the other "rides again." No wonder I loved them both.

I even loved to get scared. Well, I figured, *Inner Sanctum* couldn't frighten me any longer. I was not a kid any more. So I listened. This is from a broadcast that opens with a man shouting, "Let me go!" and crying, "You're sucking the blood out of me!" He finds himself in his bedroom, the night table has crashed to the floor, and he hears a knock at the door:

> Helen: Martin—open the door. It's Helen.
> Sound: The door opens
> Helen: Are you all right?
> Martin: Of course.
> Helen: Your face is white.
> Martin: I'm all right, I tell you. I tossed in my sleep. I knocked over the table. That's why I screamed.
> Helen: Martin, you haven't been the same ever since you returned from your South American tour . . .

It is a classic scare from my time: the hero has dared to go to an exotic location, or to try something society frowns upon. He has overreached, and there are consequences. Imagine that "South America" once conjured up something daring, even something forbidden. Will my heroes never learn? Will I ever learn not to scare myself? Apparently not, for then I heard the following on *Lights Out*:

> Narrator: Hideous things come out of the darkness to prowl the tortured earth. Evil hands stretch forth to seize. Evil eyes are watching. Unholy voices whisper and quarrel in the fearful silence. Death stalks—loathsome horrible death. Dare you put out your lights and listen to Boris Karloff in a story of horror in the deepening darkness? Dare you listen to . . . Lights Out?
> Ed: You have to be very cautious, David. I think working with monkeys is about as far as you should go right now . . .
> Ruth: David can't go any farther with animals. He's ready for the next step . . .

Of course, we all know what the next step will be as David experiments with bringing back animals from the dead.

We also knew that Clark Kent invariably would have to convince the police, or his editor, that something bad was going to happen, and he

tried hard to get them to listen to him. Kent also could not tip off anyone how he knew—although, now that I think about it, what would have
been so wrong if the whole world knew his real identity? Wouldn't it
have made crooks think twice if they knew there really was a Superman,
that he really had X-ray vision and super-hearing and could find them
any time, any place? But these are cosmic questions. I might as well ask,
Why did the Lone Ranger wear a mask? How did it really help him catch
the crooks?

> Clark Kent (speaking into phone): Mr. White? This is Clark Kent.
> Perry White (editor): Good lord, man! I thought you were dead. Where
> have you been all day?
> Kent: Tied up in a cellar. But I broke out. Listen, Mr. White—how long
> before you go to press?
> White: Now wait a minute. I'm going to press right now.
> Kent: Well, hold it—will you?
> White: This better be a good one, Kent.
> Kent: You won't regret it.
> White: What's this about a mysterious flying figure? Something called
> a Superman.
> Kent (laughing): Oh, forget it, Mr. White.

I watched *Sky King* when it moved to television. But I was struck by
how unimposing his airplane was. The mystery, and the thrill, of flight,
had been downsized to a twelve-inch screen, in black and white, as
opposed to the greater expanse of the imagination. Similarly, that
"whoosh" that signified Superman's arrival on radio never could be
matched on television as effectively as the somewhat puffy and costumed
George Reeves "landed" in front of some surprised crooks. And even *The
Lone Ranger* on television had lost the sense of place and time, almost as
if it had been ripped from the Old West, and all the possibilities of a
young America, into a world that was side-by-side with all those cheap
cowboy movies I used to see at the Miller Theater. A silver bullet never
sparkled on television the way it did on radio.

Where had Jack Armstrong gone off to? And Hop Harrigan and his
sidekick? How dare the Shadow disappear from the airwaves? What kind
of healthful breakfasts were the kids having by now? Some sugar-laced,
artificially colored product with a cutsie-poo name? But sponsors

deserted radio, and television became the world's largest advertising medium.

The kids were watching *Hawkins Falls, Pop. 6,200,* and a show starring Gabby Hayes, Roy Rogers' sidekick, *Howdy Doody* and *Captain Video* and Pinky Lee. *Sky King* and some of the others had not survived on television very long—certainly not the length of a boy's childhood. Instead, Saturday morning became the repository of children's television. Within another ten years, the shows made the transition to cartoons, which were cheaper to produce.

But the memories are palpable. Not only mine, but absent any statistic to the contrary, I daresay it is true of everyone of my generation. They couldn't tell you who sponsors *Sixty Minutes* or *Monday Night Football,* much less recite the commercials. Ah, but ask about Wheaties, or *Jack Armstrong,* and you'll get the introduction, the commercial, the names of the featured players, maybe even the names of the writers. It is why there are dozens of Web sites hawking radio trivia items or simply providing a momentary peek into the past; catalogues still selling Annie's Ovaltine shaker mug, and why I still look at a box of Cheerios and can't help thinking that they've misspelled the name. It's Cherioats, isn't it?

Other Books by Gerald Eskenazi

A Sportswriter's Life: From the Desk of a *New York Times* Reporter

Gang Green: An Irreverent Look Behind the Scenes at Thirty-Eight (Well, Thirty-Seven) Seasons of New York Jets Football Futility

Bill Veeck: A Baseball Legend

The Lip: A Biography of Leo Durocher

Yaz (with Carl Yastrzemski)

A Year on Ice

Hockey

The Fastest Sport

There Were Giants in Those Days

A Thinking Man's Guide to Pro Soccer

Hockey Is My Life (with Phil Esposito)

The Derek Sanderson Nobody Knows

A Thinking Man's Guide to Pro Hockey

Hockey for Children

Miracle on Ice (with others)

The Way It Was (with others)